Set My
Heart Free

by
Rita Carmack

Jewel Press
Windsor, Colorado

Set My Heart Free
ISBN 0-88144-031-0
Copyright © 1984 by Rita Carmack
Jewel Press
P.O. Box 2042
Windsor, Colorado 80550

Published by Jewel Press
P.O. Box 2042
Windsor, Colorado 80550

CONTENTS

ACKNOWLEDGEMENTS

I thank first the Holy Spirit who led and inspired me to write this book. Without Him it would not have been written.

Appreciation also goes to my husband, Derin; my daughter, Starlyn; and to Patsye Hurley, who read, made suggestions and encouraged me. Thanks also to Judy Kegin, who typed the first draft; to Liz Webb, who did many pages of retyping; to Bob Webb, who provided the cover photo; and to all, especially my Bible study group, who prayed for the publication of this book.

DEDICATION

This book is lovingly dedicated to my beautiful mother whose saintly life instilled within me a love for beauty and for life.

She is in heaven now, but the godly example she lived before me is still an inspiration and a spiritual influence in my life.

INTRODUCTION

This book was written because of my strong desire to see God's children find healing and freedom in every area of their lives — spiritual, mental and physical.

In my own Christian walk, I was frustrated by the sermons and books that told what I should do or be, without telling me how. In this book, I have endeavored to show you how to walk the path to freedom, peace and joy in your everyday life.

This is my prayer for you:

"In the powerful Name of Jesus I pray that the eyes of your spirit will be opened and enlightened as your read this book.

"I pray you will come to a better understanding and deeper knowledge of God and His Word. That you will realize who you really are in Christ Jesus.

"I pray also that you will use the scriptural principles taught in this book to become re-created in spirit, renewed in mind, healthy in body, prosperous in finances, and fulfilled in your relationships with others. Amen."

1
GOD'S FREE GIFT

Man's Search

Some time ago our local newspaper published an article based on the results of a national survey. The article reported that a majority of the people surveyed (over 89%) were seeking "experiences that make you peaceful inside." It concluded that "inner peace is sought by close to 9 out of 10 adults."

This same survey also pointed out that American adults placed high priority on using their creative abilities and being involved in efforts where people cooperate instead of compete.

How can people realize such goals? How can they find inner peace and freedom to develop individual creativity? What is this freedom for which they long?

Many would say that political freedom is the answer to man's quest for happiness. Yet in our "land of the free" most people are not content or truly happy.

This book contains answers about inner peace and freedom. As you read it, you can discover the most important freedom of all — spiritual freedom. This freedom is taught in the Word of God. It is freedom of man's inmost part — his spirit.

Use the ideas presented in this book and you can be free from guilt, fear, inferiority feelings, resentments, bitterness, and even grief and loneliness.

This freedom allows you to be real — not having to be on guard in your relationships with others. It will eliminate any need to be phony or to cover up your true self.

Satan wants you to think, "If people knew the real person I am, they wouldn't love or accept me." He wants to convince you that you are unworthy of God's love and of the love and trust of other people. Through a knowledge and application of God's Word you can learn how to defeat Satan in his deception. He wants you to feel worthless and unloveable, but the Bible says, *How great is the love the Father has lavished on us, that we should be called the children of God!* (1 John 3:1).

In Romans 8:38-39 Paul states: *For I am convinced that neither death, nor life, neither angels nor demons, ...nor anything else in all creation, will be able to separate us from the love of God that is in Christ Jesus our Lord.*

Isaiah says of God: *He tends his flock like a shepherd: He gathers the lambs in his arms and carries them close to his heart* (Is. 40:11).

You can see from these verses that God sees us as worthy objects of His love. Our freedom comes, then, from accepting God's view of us; not our view, or that of friends or relatives, but God's view.

The first step toward freedom is to accept God's love and forgiveness, to know Him as your Father, through Jesus Christ. This will give you a new spirit and as you follow the steps in this book, you will become free not only spiritually, but mentally and physically as well.

Christ stated, *"Then you will know the truth, and the truth will set you free"* (John 8:32).

What is this truth Jesus was talking about? The answer is threefold:

1. **God's Word:** *"Sanctify them by the truth; your word is truth"* (John 17:17). (Sanctify meaning to set apart or to make holy.)

2. **Jesus Himself:** *"I am the way and the truth and the life"* (John 14:6).
3. **The Holy Spirit:** *"But when he, the Spirit of truth, comes, he will guide you into all truth"* (John 16:13).

Our Ministry Begins

From the beginning my husband and I had a "Christian marriage." At least both of us had made a commitment to God and we had been quite faithful in church attendance. But certainly we were not at peace or free.

We moved many, many times over the first years of our marriage. Once from Seattle to Kansas and back to Seattle all in one month's time. Then my husband, Derin, finally finished college and became a successful school teacher. By then we lived in Colorado.

But Derin was not happy, so we both dropped out of the education field. In the next three or four years we went from bad to worse financially until our debts were overwhelming.

We put our beautiful, custom-built home in the country up for sale and moved into a little rental house in Kansas. By that time I had developed a measure of inner peace and joy but Derin was still searching.

At this point he had found what would seem to be a job that suited his personality perfectly. Yet he was still not happy or content.

Through a phone call to a dear friend in Seattle, Derin learned about an organization called Burden Bearers which his friend felt could help him find peace and contentment. Unfortunately, counseling appointments for the organization were booked up solid for the next two months. However, Derin was desperate, he told his friend, "I'll be there tomorrow," and he was. Of course, God had everything under control and the next day there were two appointment cancellations. A counselor met with Derin and explained to him how God could heal the hurts from his past and set him free.

Three of the staff members laid hands on Derin and prayed for fear and anger to leave him. That evening I received a call, "I've found the answer, I'm free. I'm a new person." This glowing report was met with no small amount of skepticism on my part! Many times before Derin had found "the answer" and each time the change had been brief. He would soon go back to being his "old self" again.

"Don't get your hopes up," had been my watchword for so long that I had hardly any hope left that Derin would ever really change permanently. I was more or less resigned to my "fate." I had come to accept that my place was to be a dutiful wife and to cope as well as possible with the numerous job changes, the chasing after "get-rich-quick schemes," and the frequent moves from one place to another.

Not that I did all of this without being hurt and resentful, but I had decided that I would never divorce him so I just tried to be as happy as possible in spite of circumstances!

What a happy surprise then when my husband returned home from Seattle and I could truly see a change in him! I noticed that he seemed less angry and frustrated, that he expressed more understanding and love toward me and our three children, for which we all rejoiced.

Then almost immediately, people began to come to our house seeking counsel and prayer. Sometimes it would be relatives or friends, but not infrequently people we had never met before would come to us from other towns and even from out of state. As the volume of people seeking our help grew larger and larger we soon realized that God was calling us into a ministry of reaching out to others, mostly disillusioned Christians, to help them find peace, joy, and freedom in their walk with Christ. Thus, New Creation Life* was brought into being and Derin and I started an exciting ministry together.

Christians in Bondage

Early that spring I heard a sermon that included, in the scriptures read, Mark 12:24, and that verse really became impressed on my mind: *Jesus replied, "Are you not in error because you do not know the Scriptures or the power of God?"* In this passage Jesus was telling the Sadduces how incorrect they were in their beliefs about heaven, because they didn't know (or understand) the Scriptures.

The thought occurred to me then that the same was true of many Christians I knew. They had much unbelief and error in their minds because they didn't know the Word of God!

Many church people today are arguing about and questioning things that are clearly answered in the Bible. Satan is using on them the same deceit he used on Eve: *He* (Satan) *said to the woman, "**Did God really say**, 'You must not eat from any tree in the garden'?"* (Gen. 3:1).

*Later the name of our ministry was changed to Derin Carmack Ministries.

Satan's deceit worked and Eve sinned. In today's society his deceit is causing many people to live defeated lives because he causes them to wonder and question whether the Bible, God's Word, really means what it says. This doubt and questioning causes them to live below their rights and privileges as God's children. Because of doubt and unbelief, many Christians today do not possess God's power which is available to those who know the Word and believe it.

Jesus' life and deeds while here on this earth are evidence of the truth in God's Word. Jesus fulfilled the Old Testament prophecies about the Messiah perfectly. His ministry showed God's will for men: *"For I have come down from heaven not to do my will but to do the will of him who sent me"* (John 6:38).

His ministry was salvation, healing and abundant life.

In Acts 4:12 Peter said of Jesus: *"Salvation is found in no one else, for there is no other name under heaven given to men by which we must be saved."*

Matthew tells us that *Jesus went through Galilee, teaching, ...preaching..., and healing every disease and sickness among the people* (Matt. 4:23).

And Jesus Himself declared in John 10:10: *"...I have come that they may have life, and have it to the full."*

A Way Out

So we find the truth and freedom in Jesus: *For sin shall not be your master, because you are not under law, but under grace* (Rom. 6:14).

God's favor (grace) comes to us when we accept Jesus as His Son and our Lord. As Christians our testimony is that of the Apostle Paul: *"Therefore, there is now no condemnation for those who are in Christ Jesus, because through Christ Jesus the Law of the Spirit of life **set me free** from the law of sin and death"* (Rom. 8:1-2).

Yet, I know there are many Christians today who yearn, just as I once did, to know God's power in their lives, to see Him work in and through them to help others. Perhaps that is your desire also. That is why I have written this book, knowing that God has directed me to some answers that have brought change in my own life and in the lives of many others, and that these same answers will work for you too.

First, you must believe that you are God's child and that Jesus is within you. This is a simple act. Just pray this prayer from a sincere heart:

"Lord, I repent and turn away from the sins in my life. I believe that Jesus is the Christ, the Son of the living God. I accept Him as my Savior and make Him Lord in my life. Thank You, Lord, for hearing this prayer and for forgiving my sins. Amen."

On the authority of God's Word *(...if you confess with your mouth, "Jesus is Lord," and believe in your heart that God raised him from the dead, you will be saved* (Rom. 10:9), you are now His child.

As soon as possible find opportunity to tell someone about your relationship with God. Jesus said that if we do not confess Him before men He would not confess us before His Father in heaven. (Matt. 10:33.) We must say, verbally, that Jesus is Lord in our life.

For the remainder of this book, I am going to assume that every person reading it has accepted

Christ as his or her personal Savior. If you haven't done that, then the spiritual truths presented here won't make sense to you.

Here are three verses that explain your new position before God, now that you have taken this step of faith:

For he has rescued us from the dominion of darkness and brought us into the kingdom of the Son he loves, in whom we have redemption, the forgiveness of sins.

Colossians 1:13-14

Yet to all who received him, to those who believed in his name, he gave the right to become children of God.

John 1:12

The Spirit himself testifies with our spirit that we are God's children.

Romans 8:16

God Desires Good for us

Secondly, let's establish again from God's Word that **the Lord desires good for you because you are now His child.**

Jesus told His disciples, *"If you, then, ...know how to give good gifts to your children, how much more will your Father in heaven give good gifts to those who ask him!"* (Matt. 7:11).

And again, speaking in John 10:10, Jesus says, *"...I have come that they may have life, and have it to the full* (abundantly).*"*

James tells us, *Every good and perfect gift is from above, coming down from the Father of the heavenly lights, who does not change like shifting shadows* (James 1:17).

Even nature speaks to us of God's desire that we enjoy good things. I marvel at the beauty provided in

His world. Towering mountains, blue skies with billowing clouds, flaming sunsets and the loveliness of flowers — from tiny violets to tall magnolia trees, from the first crocus of spring to the last chrysanthemum of fall — all attest to the Lord's will that we be blessed with awe-inspiring beauty.

Can you even name all the different kinds of fruits or vegetables? Their variety in color, flavor and texture is amazing. We could have probably existed on only potatoes and apples, but God "threw in" egg plants and watermelon!

How can we believe that the best is not His desire for His children? We must believe, deep within ourselves, that truly every good and perfect gift is from God and the bad things that come upon us are from Satan. We must learn to resist the bad and affirm the good.

Because we live in a sinful world and are human, even though born again, most of us will never escape having troubles and, in many cases, suffering. But we must learn that these troubles originate with Satan. How we allow God to work with us during these problem times will determine whether they become stepping stones, building Christ-like character in us and bringing glory to God, or whether we give Satan a victory by allowing the trials to cause us to doubt and become bitter toward God or other people. The choice of whether we become defeated people or overcomers is up to us.

No, in all these things we are more than conquerors through him who loved us.

Romans 8:37

*His divine power has given us everything we need for life and godliness **through our knowledge of him** who called us by his own glory and goodness. Through these he has given us his very great and precious promises, so that **through them** you may participate in the divine nature and escape the corruption in the world caused by evil desires.*

For this very reason, make every effort to add to your faith goodness; ...knowledge; ...self-control; ...perseverance; ...godliness; ...brotherly kindness; and ...love. For if you possess these qualities in increasing measure, they will keep you from being ineffective and unproductive in your knowledge of our Lord Jesus Christ.

2 Peter 1:3-8

Do you often feel ineffective and unproductive for Christ? Does that list (faith, goodness, self-control, etc.) seem like an impossibility to you? Notice that Peter says that you are to make every effort to add these virtues and to possess them in increasing measure. This is not a magic trick in which God zaps you with all the knowledge and love you'll ever need in one great experience. Notice these two key statements: "**Through our knowledge of Him** (Jesus)", and, "He has given us His great and precious promises, so that **through them** (the great and precious promises of His Word) you may participate in the divine nature..."

This is the truth which I am presenting in this book: How you can make your efforts fruitful — through knowledge of God's ways and through having His promises, the Word, in your spirit. It is not my purpose to describe **what you should do and be;** you have heard plenty of sermons and read much about that. Rather, it is my goal to help you learn **how you can** do the correct things to achieve spiritual growth and stability. Then you can be a radiant, joyful, whole Christian attracting others to Jesus and His love.

Prayer

"**Dear Lord, I pray that the eyes of my heart and spirit be enlightened as I read this book and Your words that are in it. Through application of the truths that it contains, may I be strengthened and encouraged. Help me to grow spiritually and become free in my inner being so I can reach out and be a giver of love, helping people around me.**

"**In the loving Name of Jesus, Amen.**"

2

BECOMING A HARMONIOUS PERSON

A New Spirit

The most frequently heard criticism of Christians today is that we are hypocrites. And sad to say, I have to admit that far too many of us are. Why is this so?

It is because our spirit, mind, and body are not whole and in harmony one with the other. There is much ignorance about the spirit part of our being. There is much neglect in the area of our mind and emotions. There is much unbelief concerning our bodies.

This whole book is dedicated to enlightening you about God's will and ways for all three parts of your being. This chapter is just a sort of overview. The rest of the book will guide you and tell you how to become a person who is not phony in any way. As a friend of mine says, "You will be a 'well-put-together' person."

Therefore, if anyone is in Christ, he is a new creation; the old has gone, the new has come!

2 Corinthians 5:17

According to this verse, *anyone* who is in Christ is a new creation. Anyone must mean you and me and everyone who has accepted Jesus.

"But I don't understand," you may say. "If anyone means me, if I am supposed to be a new person in Christ, then how come my temper still flares, why do I still find it hard to forgive people who wrong me, why do I still have to take tranquilizers to relieve my tension?''

This verse is not talking about your being a new person physically, or mentally, or emotionally. It means that you are a new person spiritually. The Bible has much to say about our heart and spirit. Most of us have heard a great deal about our minds and bodies, but little, if any, teaching about our heart and spirit. Here is a verse that will help you to better understand your spirit:

The spirit of a man [that factor in human personality which proceeds immediately from God] is the lamp of the Lord, searching all his innermost parts.

Proverbs 20:27 AMP

Instead of using our mind (psychology) to try to find the root of our problems, we should use spiritual insight, the lamp (light) of the Lord which can search our innermost parts.

More and more our society is finding that psychiatry and medical treatment are not enough to solve man's frustrations and illnesses. To be truly whole and well, we must have the healing light of God applied to our heart and spirit because it is there that we find the root of most of our problems.

By accepting God's forgiveness and cleansing you can receive a new spirit within you, the Spirit of Christ. In Matthew 21:42 Jesus is referred to as the cornerstone. By building upon that foundation, using the tools of prayer, the Word and the ways of God, you can become a truly whole and harmonious person.

In Christ we have a new spirit created within us. But in most cases that does not instantly make us new and whole in our mind (emotions and attitudes) or body (habits and physical weaknesses). These must be brought into harmony with our new spiritual being.

A Transformed Mind

So, after our spirit is made new, we must go on to the instruction found in Romans 12:2: *Do not conform any longer to the pattern of this world, but be transformed by the renewing of your mind.*

A transformation is a real and dramatic change; like the metamorphosis of a caterpillar from a multi-legged creature, crawling from leaf to leaf, to a butterfly flitting on iridescent wings from flower to flower.

I'm sure God wants His children to no longer creep from problem to problem, barely able to survive, but rather He wants us to wing our way in freedom and joy from victory to victory!

If this is not the case, what do we have to offer our hurting world? They know what it is to be struggling with problems. If they are going to give up their worldly fun (as fleeting as it may be) and "ruin" their weekends by going to church on Sunday, they must see in the Christian's life an answer and a reason for committment to Christ.

I was once a part of a witnessing team. We were talking to a man, trying to lead him to Christ. His reaction? "Why should I become a Christian? I'm happy with my life like it is. We are dong fine financially, our children aren't giving us a problem, we are all healthy. Everything is great. Now the guy next door, he's a Christian. He has all kinds of problems, money troubles, sickness... why would I want to become a Christian?''

Why indeed? None of our witness group had an answer.

A Whole Body

I am saying it is God's will that, as His children, we be blessed and protected in our spirits (new creations), in our minds (joyful), and in our bodies (healthy). Most church people today accept that God does change the spiritual part of us when we come to Him, and they agree that our attitudes and habits (mind-controlled things) should change, but they seem to have difficulty accepting that God also provides for healthy bodies.

I am the mother of three children. Do I want them sick? Never. And I try to see that they get proper nutrition and rest so that they stay healthy. Do I love my children more than God loves His children? Certainly not! So, common logic tells me that God wants us well in our bodies.

God's desire for our well-being also includes financial blessings. If my children need money for school supplies, clothes or lunch, I am happy to provide it. I even like to go a step further and give them some things they desire but don't necessarily need. God enjoys giving to us also.

Don't just take my word for it. Look at His Word:

Beloved, I wish above all things that thou mayest prosper and be in health, even as thy soul prospereth.

3 John 2 KJV

Matthew, quoting from Isaiah 53:4, says of Jesus, *He took our sicknesses away and carried our diseases for us* (Matt. 8:17 *Jerusalem Bible*).

If Christ took our sicknesses away and carried our

diseases for us, then why should we still be carrying them around?

In 2 Corinthians 8:9 Paul writes: *For you know the grace of our Lord Jesus Christ, that though he was rich, yet for your sakes he became poor, so that you through his poverty might become rich.*

Many well-meaning but doubtful Christians to whom I quote this verse are quick to point out that they interpret it to mean that we are to be *spiritually* rich. My question to them is, did Christ become spiritually impoverished in His earthly life? If He, who was sinless and perfect in His attitude toward God, was spiritually poor we had better give up right now. There is no hope for any of us. No. Christ wasn't poor in that way — He was poor in material possessions. Is there any indication that this verse changes meaning, right in the middle, from material things, in Christ's case, to spiritual things, in our case? Not that I can find!

(I'll give more detail and scripture about health and prosperity in later chapters.)

God's Word — Our Proof

I don't know who first said this, but it is a quote some Christians may do well to ponder: "If God didn't mean what He said, why didn't He say what He meant?"

Let's quit looking for what we think are inconsistencies in the Word of God. Let's quit looking for ways to twist God's Word to make it support our unbelief. Let's try a new way — accepting the Word for what it says. We need to learn not to base our faith on personal experiences or hearsay — what we have seen or failed to see in our own lives and the lives of others — but rather solely upon the Word of God.

The argument that healing or prosperity is not God's will because So-and-So was such a wonderful saint and got sick, or went bankrupt, or died, or whatever, should never shake our faith. **God's will is not determined by what happens to Christians, it is determined by His infallible Word!**

Our faith then is based not on feelings or experiences but on the Word of God which we memorize and meditate on day and night. We let it become a vital part of our being, renewing our minds, healing our bodies, establishing faith, knowledge and power within us.

Then we are transformed by God's love rather than being conformed to today's popular religious unbeliefs. As we believe and confess the Word of God, that Word becomes true in our own personal lives.

What if some did not have faith? Will their lack of faith nullify God's faithfulness? Not at all! Let God be true, and every man a liar.

Romans 3:3-4

My son, pay attention to what I (God) say; listen closely to my words. Do not let them out of your sight, keep them within your heart; for they are life to those who find them and health to a man's whole body.

Proverbs 4:20-23

Prayer

"I pray to You, God, my Father, that You would help me as I study and work to become a whole and harmonious person. May my spirit, mind and body be healed, restored, and disciplined to walk in Your ways at all times. Reveal to me the Truth that is in Your Word that I may be set free.

"In Jesus' Name, Amen."

3

A GLIMPSE OF FREEDOM

A Spiritual Journey

I started getting glimpses of what was possible in the Lord a few years ago while reading a book entitled *I Will Lift Up Mine Eyes* written by Glenn Clark.[1]

This book was so positive. Over and over the author told how God's Word had affected his life and the lives of others in wonderful, exciting ways. He talked about how we develop ''hind's feet'' so we can walk in high places. (Ps. 18:33.) He explained that this was done through getting our subconscious and conscious minds in perfect alignment and agreement with each other and also with God's will. The joy, security, the oneness with God, the miracles which Glenn Clark related in his book made me want these things in my life too.

Also, because Glenn Clark mentioned Agnes Sanford in his books, I began reading her writings. (Mrs. Sanford was a respected Christian author whose books I highly reccommend.) Once again, I saw presented a beautiful way of living that intrigued me.

In reviewing their books now I find that these two authors used affirmations or positive confessions and suggested that the reader do likewise. But somehow at that time I didn't fully understand this principle or realize that it needed to be done every day over a period of time in order to effectively change my old

[1]Harper & Row Publishers, New York, 1937

thought patterns and renew my mind.

So, I am going to explain specifically how to renew your mind so that your Christian life is victorious, with Christ working in and through you.

These ideas have been successful for my husband and me and for those with whom we have counseled. I am confident they will also be successful for you!

Healed from Depression

Early in our ministry Derin and I counseled with a man we'd never met before our first session with him. Bill*, himself a Christian minister, had trouble with fear and deep depression. From early childhood his subconscious mind had been programmed to fear by both his mother and his religious teachings.

Bill had a super-sensitive spirit that picked up fear signals as readily as faith signals. Unfortunately, most of the religious teaching he had received had taught fear instead of faith.

Bill had been to four Christian counselors, three of whom were psychiatrists. They gave him truth serum and found some of the reasons for his fears, but their best advice was to ''relax.''

This didn't really help Bill at all. Finally the last psychiatrist, in conjunction with a medical doctor, gave him a mood-elevating drug. He also advised him to relax and to give up his pastorate in the church.

Bill took the medication for two years and was all right as long as he took it. However, he was troubled

*Names have been changed throughout this book to protect privacy.

by the inconsistency of preaching to people that Jesus was the answer to their problems when he couldn't face life himself without taking pills.

Also, the pills were supposed to have cured him in a year. So Bill decided he would pray, expect God to help him, and quit taking his medication. As soon as he went off the mood-elevating drugs, he went back into deep depression, and almost total despair. He felt extremely tired, and when he lay down he felt as though he never wanted to get up again.

Bill decided to go back on the medication, get out of his pastorate, and take a secular job. He decided he could support other ministries financially rather than try to minister to others personally.

The day he came to see us, Bill had already lined up a job in another state and was looking for housing there.

He did not want to see any more counselors and did not expect our counseling to be of any help to him. I suppose he only came because his wife kept urging him, saying, "It can't hurt anything." And, his curiosity was aroused when my husband said to him, "I can help you and I can tell you why the other counselors didn't help you."

When I called Bill to ask him if I could use his story in my book, he said, "Yes, and tell them I am *well*."

Then he went on to say, "I never thought I could ever be well and independent, not having to have someone to always prop me back up. I don't need that now because the Word does it continuously."

Not only is Bill well personally, but his ministry has been blessed in a beautiful way. Through it he has seen many people healed spiritually, mentally, and physically.

It would have literally been a disaster if Satan had been allowed to block Bill's dynamic ministry through fear and depression.

The things I am sharing with you in this book are the same things we shared with Bill — plus (since he was one of the first people we ever counseled) many new insights the Lord has given my husband and me since that time.

Man's Three Parts

The Bible talks about the three parts of man: spirit, mind (or soul), and body (or flesh).

When we accept Jesus as Lord, we are born again in our spirit. (Read Christ's explanation of this to Nicodemus in the third chapter of the Gospel of John.) Spiritually we become a new creation: *Therefore, if anyone is in Christ, he is a new creation; the old has gone, the new has come!* (2 Cor. 5:17).

Our problems come in on the mind and body levels. Old emotional and physical habits seldom miraculously disappear overnight. This, then, is where we must renew ourselves, using the Word of God as the tool. *"Then you will know the truth, and the truth will set you free"* (John 8:32).

We will start now doing things in the order God intended. Being sure first that we have a new spirit, then renewing our minds in His Word, and then expecting to see our lives, our relationships with others, our families, marriages and physical bodies healed.

King David had the right order in Psalm 51 where he first prayed for a pure heart and a renewed spirit (v. 10.), then for the joy of God's salvation (new emotions — mind area) (v. 12.), and then declared that his mouth and lips (body) would proclaim God's praise (vs. 14-15.).

We modern people usually go about this healing process backwards; treating our bodies for illnesses, expecting that when we feel better physically it will cure our mental problems and somehow even affect us spiritually. Physicians will tell you that up to 90% of people's illnesses are a result of wrong emotions and poor mental attitudes.

So we find that the false philosophies of today's society ("Do your own thing," "If it feels good, do it," and "situation ethics") don't work (today's divorce and suicide rates are proof of that!) and never will. God's ways, not man's, contain the answers we seek.[2]

The Apostle Paul tells us in Colossians 2:8: *See to it that no one takes you captive through hollow and deceptive philosophy, which depends on human tradition and the basic principles of this world rather than on Christ.*

Then in 1 Corinthians 2:4-5 Paul says that his preaching was not with wise words but with a demonstration of the Spirit's power so that the faith of those to whom he preached the Gospel would not depend

---

[2]For a thoughtful, in-depth analysis of how man's philosophies have not worked historically or in today's society, I suggest you read *How Should We Then Live?* by Francis Schaeffer, Fleming H. Revell Co., Old Tappan, N.J., 1976.

on man's wisdom, but on God's power.

Finally, in 2 Timothy 3:16-17 Paul states, *All Scripture is God-breathed and is useful for teaching, rebuking, correcting and training in righteousness, so that the man of God may be thoroughly equipped for every good work.*

Prayer

"Dear Lord, I want Your peace, joy and freedom to be within me. I know that man's answers will not be a solution to my problems. Your Word, Lord, is what contains life, healing and wholeness. Help me to walk daily in Your ways. May the Word become an integral part of my total being.

"I choose to base my whole life on what Your Word teaches rather than on man's philosophies. Thank You, Lord, for enabling me to do this.

"In the powerful Name of Jesus, Amen."

4

FREEDOM FROM THE PAST

Pulling Out the "Splinters"

I am an antique buff. I enjoy taking old pieces of furniture and stripping, sanding and rubbing them with oil until they are smooth and beautiful. Now anyone who has worked much with wood knows that sometimes splinters from it will go into your fingers. As long as the splinter is left in the flesh there will be pain when you accidentally hit it or push against it. If left long enough, infection can set in. If not properly cared for, a serious problem can develop.

There are many Christians today who are suffering from spiritual "splinters," unresolved hurts or guilts that are causing them pain because they don't know how to let God come into their spirit and/or subconscious mind and remove the source of the problem. Perhaps that is your situation. Unpleasant memories, guilt, hurt feelings and resentment from the past are a cause of pain every time Satan brings them to mind. If not removed through a prayer of release they can inhibit or destroy your joy in your daily Christian walk.

However, if you will let go of these past hurtful incidents, allowing God to pull out all the "splinters," and then use the truth from the Word to renew your mind, you can become completely free in spirit, mind and body.

In Matthew 9:2-8 we find the story of Christ healing a paralyzed man. First Jesus forgave the man's sins (causing the Pharisees to criticize Him). Then to

31

demonstrate that He had power to forgive and to heal, He said to the man, *"Get up, take your mat and go home"* (v. 6).

In John 14:12 Jesus says, *"...anyone who has faith in me will do what I have been doing. He will do even greater things than these, because I am going to the Father."*

How many Christians do you know who are doing what Jesus did; boldly teaching God's ways, healing people, performing miracles? Not only have most of us not been doing that, we haven't even seemed to be concerned about it. Why is this? Don't we believe that Jesus meant what He said? Or are we too confused and burdened down by our own guilts, fears and resentments, working so hard to get ourselves put together, that we don't have the time and energy to do as Jesus did?

For many Christians I think the last suggested answer is more accurate. We are like Bill in the last chapter, fearful and depressed, hurting so much ourselves that we are unable to reach out and help others.

Bill's depression was mostly, if not all, a result of guilts and fears that had been placed on him during his childhood. When we prayed for the healing of those memories, he quit taking medication and is now a joyful and productive Christian.

Psychology books tell us that 90% of the human mind is comprised of the subconscious. Only about 10% of our mind is devoted to conscious thinking, reasoning, goal setting.

From birth to about age five or six, we have not yet formed our own self-concept so our estimation of ourselves is based on the attitudes and actions of others with whom we come in contact. Up to this point we accept what parents, relatives, teachers, and other adults say or do to us as a true indication of who we are.

Therefore, undeserved punishment, scoldings and negative statements such as "Bad boy," "Naughty girl," "You'll never amount to anything," "How can you be so stupid?" "Won't you ever learn?" "Clumsy!" "You're dumb!" go into our subconscious computer and register a feeling of rejection. These often produce a low self-concept that is apt to stay with us a life-time.

Some people, like me, are very blessed in having had a secure and happy childhood. But others, like many we have counseled, have childhood memories that are very hurtful, leaving them feeling rejected and worthless.

But everyone, even those with almost perfect childhoods, have had, at some time or another in their lives, negative inputs that have hurt or angered them. Hurts that have come from peers or teachers in school or from churches or pastors who emphasize the judgement and wrath of God. And, of course, many hurts come from marriage situations.

For years the average person has heard these kinds of statements: "Your daddy/mommy didn't really love us or he/she wouldn't have left us"; "When your dad finds out what you did, you're really going to get it"; "God won't love you if you're bad"; "If you don't behave, the boogie man will get you"; "Shame on you for doing that"; and, "Don't play in the street, you'll get run over and *killed*!"

Also, there are the things we did in the past, the

sins we committed, the embarrassment or shame or guilt (real or imagined) that we have suffered, which all have a negative effect upon us.

So it isn't any wonder that, as adults, we struggle with fears, depression, resentments, guilt and poor self-concepts. We read books on positive thinking, maybe go to a psychiatrist or group therapy meeting. We find out what our hang-ups are and perhaps some reasons why we have them. We are told what kind of people we should be, but we can't seem to bridge the gap between what we think we are and what we want to become.

Prayer for Healing
Therefore confess your sins (faults) *to each other and pray for each other so that you may be healed. The prayer of a righteous man is powerful and effective.*

James 5:16

Using this verse as a directive, take a piece of paper and make a list of all the sins that have caused you a problem, both current ones and those of the past that you still "hold against" yourself.

Include on your list people who have hurt you, cheated you or lied to you. (Don't overlook family members.) List things that cause you worry or fear. Put down things about yourself, physical or personality traits or lack of abilities, that you have trouble accepting.

Many people like to have two lists, one that they can feel free to share with a trusted friend, counselor or pastor, and another private list to be prayed over (without discussion) and destroyed.

Share the first list with whomever you've decided can help you in this healing process.* Discuss any parts you feel need to be talked over or clarified. Actually if they were important enough to be remembered and written down, it is good to talk about all of them because verbalizing (confessing) our problems helps us to reach the solution to them and receive healing.

After discussing your list, have your prayer partner stand behind you, placing his hands on your shoulders, as you sit in a relaxed position. (Put your hands open, palms up, signifying release of the past and acceptance of what God wants to give you to replace that past. His desire is that you receive forgiveness, freedom and healing.)

Then, using your first list as a guide, your intercessor can pray for you something like this:

"Dear Lord, I come to You in the Name of Jesus Christ, Your Son. _____ and I agree that You are going to do a new thing in his/her life today, and we praise and thank You for that.

"We go back now into _____'s past, even before birth, and we ask that any negative emotions that may have been in his/her mother that affected _____ will be healed and erased by Your healing light. May the trauma or pain of the birth process

---

*If there is absolutely no one that you feel you can share your list with, then ask Jesus to be your agreeing intercessor and pray the following prayer aloud for yourself.

be erased and eased also.

"I ask that You go back into
_____'s memories and heal all the
wounds from the hurtful things that happened to him/her as he/she was growing up
in those formative years. Cause _____
to know that You were there at those times
and that now that You have healed those
memories they will no longer cause him/her
any pain or distress.

(At this point, your intercessor should specifically
mention childhood and adult hurts that are on your
list. For example:)

"Christ, You were there when
_____'s mother said that his/her
conception was an accident. You, Jesus,
longed to hold and comfort this little child
when he/she was punished so severely for
the broken window that wasn't his/her fault.

"Your heart was broken too, Jesus,
when _____ witnessed his/her father
beating his/her mother. You longed to protect, reassure and comfort _____ during
those times of hurt and fear.

"Jesus, step back in time and heal the
hurts and embarrassments _____
experienced during his/her school years.
Flow forgiveness through to the teachers and
fellow classmates who made unkind
remarks.

"Let _____ see and know in his/her
spirit that You, Lord, have always loved

him/her and planned for him/her from the foundation of the earth.

"And now, as an adult, _____ has had hurts in his/her marriage. Flow Your divine forgiveness from Christ through _____ to _____ causing him/her to forgive completely and to release _____.

"In the job situation, Jesus, _____ has been taken advantage of and used. We flow divine forgiveness from Jesus through _____ to his/her superior and he/she is releasing that person right now so there is no longer any bitterness or resentment in the relationship.

Now you pray aloud and ask God to forgive the wrong ways you reacted to these past situations. Take all anger, bitterness, resentment, guilt, fear and/or hurt feelings in these situations to the cross and ask forgiveness and cleansing of your attitudes. Thank Jesus that He has done this for you and that you are now forgiven, cleansed, free and whole in Him.

At this point many people feel a wonderful release, but if you don't, do not be discouraged. Remember, we base our faith on the Word of God, not on our feelings. The Word says, *"Again, I tell you that if two of you on earth agree about anything you ask for, it will be done for you by my Father in heaven"* (Matt. 18:19).

In John 20, Jesus gave His disciples authority to forgive sins, and James 5 tells us that we will be healed when we pray for one another. God's Word is true. Stand firmly on it.

Job 11:15-18 explains beautifully what takes place

through this kind of prayer:

"*...then you will lift up your face without shame; you will stand firm and without fear.*

"*You will surely forget your trouble, recalling it only as waters gone by.*

"*Life will be brighter than noonday, and darkness will become like morning.*

"*You will be secure, because there is hope; you will look about you and take your rest in safety.*"

Read these verses from Job aloud several times allowing them to sink deep into your spirit.

Renewing the Mind

Now your subconscious mind has been healed and cleansed from the past. Your spirit is re-created and made new. You can now go on to "being transformed by the renewing of your mind." (Rom.12:2.)

Old thought habits (automatic thought patterns engraved in your subconscious mind) have left. These thought habits must be replaced with new positive thought patterns. Your mind must be reprogrammed, renewed.

You do this by taking each of the bad thought patterns or habits and finding out its positive opposite. Then write a positive affirmation or confession about it.

Your affirmation is what you affirm the truth to be. According to Webster's dictionary, to affirm means "to *say* positively, declare firmly, or assert to be true." If you like the word confession better, Webster says that to confess means "to declare one's faith in."

After writing out your positive affirmation or confession, link it up with Bible verses that show God's point of view about His children.

Repeat these affirmations or confessions out loud twice a day, morning and evening, three times each, along with three or more Bible verses. You need to do this for at least three weeks. I repeated my initial affirmations every day for forty days, forty being a strong Biblical number that I felt had spiritual significance.

You will find that this positive affirmation of God's Word will change your life. In Isaiah 55:11 God says, *"...so is my word that goes out from my mouth: It will not return to me empty..."*

Job 22:28 declares, *You will also decree a thing, and it will be established for you; and light will shine on your ways (NAS).*

You will be saying positive things about yourself in agreement with truth, God's Word.

If you are a person who has been fearful and you are now saying, "Christ within gives me confidence in all situations," don't feel you are saying something that isn't true. You are doing things God's way. God *calls things that are not as though they were* (Rom. 4:17). God's way is right for us too, and the wonderful thing about it is — it works. The things that are not, soon come to be!

In the following chapters you will find examples of affirmations and how they have worked in different people's lives. Remember, agree with God's Word by speaking it daily. Get it into your spirit by saying it out loud.

(Our ministry provides a packet of cards with the affirmations taught about in this book, plus many others. See the end of the book for ordering instructions.)

Prayer

"Lord, I have given You all the hurts from my past. Thank You for healing my spirit and setting me free. Help me as I renew my mind to be free from all bitterness so that Satan will have no hold on me in any area of my life.

"Thank You that I will walk in total victory, overcoming all that Satan tries to bring against me. I praise You that I am more than a conqueror in Christ Jesus!

"In His Name I pray, Amen."

5

FREEDOM THROUGH FORGIVENESS

In the last chapter we touched briefly on forgiveness. Since forgiveness is so very basic and important to your Christian walk, I want to give you some suggestions and guidance in this area.

God's Word on Forgiveness

In the sixth chapter of Matthew, Jesus was teaching His disciples how they should pray. One of the things He instructed them to say was, *Forgive us our debts, as we forgive our debtors* (v. 12 *KJV*).

We know this is a very important phrase because it is the only one in the entire prayer which Jesus commented on after giving it to them. In verses 14 and 15 He told them: *"For if you forgive men when they sin against you, your heavenly Father will also forgive you. But if you do not forgive men their sins, your Father will not forgive your sins."*

Have you ever considered the fact that if you pray the Lord's Prayer with unforgiveness in your heart, without having forgiven your "debtors," then you are asking God not to forgive you? This is pretty serious! In fact, if you are walking in unforgiveness it would be best for you to remain silent when that phrase of the prayer is repeated.

Your unforgiveness blocks God's forgiveness to you! It also blocks His love from being manifested in and through you. It blocks your prayers from being

41

answered. It keeps you from hearing correctly from God. This is very clear: If we desire God's forgiveness, we must forgive others. For most people, if not all, this is humanly impossible. The only way we can truly forgive is to allow *God's* forgiveness to flow through us to those who have hurt or wronged us.

Forgiving Others

As Catherine Marshal wrote in her book *Something More*,[3] the first step to forgiveness is to clear up the past, to *forgive, if ye have ought against any: that your Father also which is in heaven may forgive you your trespasses* (Mark 11:25 *KJV*).

As we live in this world, it is inevitable that people will wrong us. Forgiveness must flow to them. Mothers, fathers, grandparents, brother, sisters — any and all relatives (including in-laws!) against whom you have "ought" — must be forgiven. After forgiving them you must then go on to teachers, school friends, professors, pastors, church leaders, employers, fellow employees, the "government," the police — anyone toward whom you may have carried any resentment.

(Forgiveness toward husbands, wives and children will be dealt with in Chapter 9.)

Now you may not *feel* like forgiving. Resentment and anger, even bitterness, may have become a way of life for you. Therefore your feelings may not be ones of forgiveness and release. The good news is that you don't have to *feel* like it to forgive someone! **You forgive as an act of your will and by the words you say.** Then your attitudes will change because God is now free to

[3]Fleming H. Revell Co., Old Tappan, N.J., 1974

help you.

You forgive by saying: "Father God, as an act of my will I forgive _____ right now. I release all anger and resentment toward _____ and I allow Your forgiveness to flow through me to him/her. Thank You for taking my anger away and replacing it with peace and love."

You can include the whole list of people you need to forgive in those blank spaces. Usually there are a few people who stand out in your mind and emotions as the ones who have hurt you most. Be sure to name them and release them.

Forgiving Yourself

Next you need to forgive and release yourself. Most of us have been taught that we are to forgive others, so we really try to do so. But many times Satan tricks us into condemning ourselves. The devil likes to bring to our minds past sins, mistakes and embarrassing situations to try to make us feel guilty or inferior. Remember, when you ask forgivenes for a sin, God forgives and *forgets,* removes that sin completely. Since God has forgotten the sin, you can be sure He is not the one who is making you think about it again. Therefore it must be Satan who is bringing it to your mind. Resist the devil and remind him that your sins are washed away by the blood of Jesus!

Forgiving God

Lastly, you need to forgive and release God. Many people have trouble admitting they have ever been angry with God, but in reality many have been and still are. Satan has tricked us into blaming tragedies on God, when in truth the devil is the one who comes to steal, kill, and destroy, while Jesus comes to give us abundant life. (John 10:10.)

When we sin, God doesn't send bad things into our life to "teach us a lesson." Rather the sin we've committed leaves an open door so that Satan can come in and cause trouble. Often Satan gets "legal right" to came against us because of our negative words, our talking the way the world talks instead of speaking the truth of God's Word.

Have you ever said, "I think I'm catching the flu," instead of saying, *"The Lord will keep* (me) *free from every disease"* (Deut. 7:15)?

It is very difficult for most of us to admit our troubles are our own doing. Instead, the tendency is to blame God. When something happens to us that does not agree with what the Word says is God's will for His children, if we go ahead and say it is God's will, then we lose our absolute!

God does not send sickness — there isn't any in heaven for Him to send! *We* allow sickness, which the devil desires to put on us, because we are weak in our Word level concerning health.

The Word says: *Don't be deceived, my dear brothers. Every good and perfect gift is from above, coming down from the Father of the heavenly lights, who does not change like shifting shadows* (James 1:16-17). Do you really believe this? If not, you leave yourself open to deception and troubles sent by Satan.

A Forgiveness Prayer

Here is a prayer you can pray that will establish forgiveness to others, yourself and God:

"Father, as an act of my will, I allow Your perfect forgiveness to flow through me to everyone who has ever hurt, disappointed or angered me in any way in my life."
(Name specifically those who come to mind here because they are the ones who are probably the object and cause of any bitterness you may have.)

"I release all unforgiveness, resentment and bitterness to You and I say that they are replaced with Your love. Forgive me, Father, for all wrong attitudes and cleanse me from them.

"I accept Your forgiveness, Lord, for all my sins and mistakes, and I release and forgive myself. I no longer hold myself in contempt, condemnation or false guilt. I will seek to know who I really am based on Your Word.

"Forgive me, Father God, for blaming You for any problems or hurts in my life. I forgive and release You and ask that a perfect understanding and love for You be established in my life.

"Thank You, Lord! In Jesus' Name, Amen."

Now affirm this:

I have forgiven completely others, myself and God, and I walk in love.

Confess:

Be kind and compassionate to one another, forgiving each other, just as in Christ God forgave you (Eph. 4:32).

Whoever loves his brother [believer] abides (lives) in the Light, and in It or in him there is no occasion for stumbling or cause for error or sin (1 John 2:10 *AMP*).

...aquit and forgive and release (give up resentment, let it drop), and you will be acquitted and forgiven and released (Luke 6:37 *AMP*).

...we know and rely on the love God has for us (1 John 4:16).

I have received some criticism concerning this teaching about forgiving God. People say, ''God has never done anything wrong. He is sinless. He doesn't need forgiveness.''

It is true that God has never sinned or made a mistake, but you may have felt He has. The problem isn't what God has done, but rather your perception of Him.

If you are angry with a friend who you feel has wronged you, even though he really has not, you still need to forgive him. He may be completely innocent, but if you are hostile or bitter toward that individual, you must forgive him before your relationship with him can be healed.

This same principle applies to your relationship with God. Your forgiveness of Him is for *your* spiritual and emotional healing — not His!

Proverbs 19:3 says, *The foolishness of man subverts his way [ruins his affairs]; then his heart is resentful and frets against the Lord (AMP).*

6

FREEDOM TO LOVE YOURSELF

A Good Self-Concept

The most prevalent problem my husband and I encounter in our counseling is that of poor self-concept. Many, many people are unsure of themselves, afraid of rejection by others. This insecurity affects every area of their lives: their marriage, their friendships and their relationship with God.

It is very difficult for anyone who does not love himself to believe in and accept the love of his spouse, his friends or even God.

"I'm having trouble loving my husband," said Jean, as she sat at my kitchen table one day.

"Do you like yourself?" I asked.

"No, I don't!"

"When you dislike yourself it is very seldom, if ever, possible to love and relate to others as God would have you. First I will help you know who you are in Christ Jesus so you can have a right concept and good feeling about yourself. Then you will be free to love others as God would have you to."

What powerful deceit Satan has used on God's children, making them think that humility and putting themselves down as worthless "worms" were one and the same thing! True humility is having a right concept of who God is and who we are in the God-man relationship. Satan has used this concept of unworthiness to keep us from being able to witness to others, from realizing our authority in Christ, and

47

from reaching our potential as God's children.

Let's look together in God's Word to see who you really are!

You are a special creation, made in God's image, loved by Him, and planned for and chosen *before the foundation of the world* (Eph. 1:4 *KJV*).

If you have an inferiority complex or trouble accepting yourself, affirm this:

God loves me unconditionally, therefore I love and accept myself unconditionally.

In Jeremiah 31:3 God declares: *"I have loved you with an everlasting love; I have drawn you with loving-kindness."*

How great is the love the Father has lavished on us, that we should be called the children of God! (1 John 3:1).

This is how God showed his love among us: He sent his one and only Son into the world that we might live through Him (1 John 4:9).

"...you whom I have upheld since you were conceived, and have carried since your birth. Even to your old age and gray hairs I am he, I am he who will sustain you" (Is. 46:3-4).

You Are Unique

Also affirm:

I don't devalue myself because I enjoy being the unique person God made me to be.

Don't you know that you yourselves are God's temple and that God's Spirit lives in you? ...God's temple is sacred, and you are that temple (1 Cor. 3:16-17).

It was you (God) who created my inmost self, and put me together in my mother's womb; for all these mysteries I thank you: for the wonder of myself, for the wonder of your works (Ps. 139:13-14 *Jerusalem Bible*).

In Luke 12, Jesus gives the illustration of how God doesn't forget even the sparrows. Then He asks His disciples if they are not worth more than many sparrows. He was telling them that God cared for and knew all about them. He told them that even the hairs of their heads were numbered!

At the moment you were conceived, God had thousands of options as to what kind of person would be created. He certainly was not limited to creating you, exactly as you are — but He did. God had and has a purpose and design for you — who you are and what you will do and become in your lifetime.

Your responsibility is not to be unhappy over the ways you may feel that God "cheated" you. Your calling is to find God's plan for you and how He wants to bless and use the person you really are!

Never put yourself down. There is a little saying I've seen printed up and hung on walls which says: "God don't make no junk." That is true. You are precious in His sight. He does not ever condemn you. He just says, "Let Me show you a better way."

Glenn Clark in *I Will Lift Up Mine Eyes* explains our uniqueness and our acceptance of that uniqueness this way:

"I believe that our sincere desires are placed in our hearts, are molded and fashioned there by the hand of God.

"...what a person seeks and craves, other things being equal, is something that is good for him, something which God intended for him to have, provided he can take it in a way that will

do no violence to any accepted moral or social code.''[4]

Self-Confidence

If you have lacked self-confidence and have been fearful or shy, affirm:

I have confidence because Christ is within me.

The Lord is my light and my salvation — whom shall I fear? (Ps. 27:1).

''Be strong and courageous. Do not be afraid..., for the Lord your God goes with you; he will never leave you nor forsake you'' (Deut. 31:6).

In him (Christ Jesus) and through faith in him we may approach God with freedom and confidence (Eph. 3:12).

So do not throw away your confidence; it will be richly rewarded (Heb. 10:35).

For God did not give us a spirit of timidity, but a spirit of power, of love and of self-discipline (2 Tim. 1:7).

God wants you to be confident in Him. He desires that you have absolute assurance that you are His special, beloved child and that you have His favor in your life.

The worldly person admires people who show confidence in themselves and what they are doing. We can draw such a person to Christ with our inner spirit of humble, quiet confidence.

Inner Peace

If you have been a nervous, anxious person, make this affirmation:

Because Jesus is in me I have peace and

[4]Page 44

contentment deep within.

Jesus said: *"I have told you these things, so that in me you may have peace"* (John 16:33).

Cast all your anxiety on him because he cares for you (1 Pet. 5:7).

Therefore, since we have been justified through faith, we have peace with God through our Lord Jesus Christ (Rom. 5:1).

Again Jesus said: *"Come to me, all you who are weary and burdened, and I will give you rest"* (Matt. 11:28).

"Be still and know that I am God" (Ps. 46:10).

Lord, when doubts fill my mind, when my heart is in turmoil, quiet me and give me renewed hope and cheer (Ps. 94:19 *TLB*).

To develop this inner peace, you must take time for quietness in your life, time when you are completely alone with God. That means time when there is no radio or television, record or tape playing. All these things may be good, but I feel it is even possible to listen to too many Christian programs. Nothing should replace the time you spend each day quietly reading God's Word, meditating on it and praying.

I realize this is very difficult for mothers with small children still at home all day. But if it is done early or late while they are in bed, or while they are taking a nap, the effort is worth the rich benefits gained.

Christ Himself often went off alone into the wilderness or mountains to pray. He knew the necessity of quiet communication with God.

A peaceful inner spirit pays dividends in physical health and beauty, in emotional stability and spiritual maturity.

And the peace of God, which transcends all understanding, will guard your hearts and your minds in Christ Jesus (Phil. 4:7).

Your beauty... should be that of your inner self, the unfading beauty of a gentle and quiet spirit, which is of great worth in God's sight (1 Pet. 3:3-4).

It is not unusual for an old acquaintance that I haven't seen for several years to comment that I'm more beautiful today than I was before. To a lady in her mid-forties that is a nice compliment to hear. However, I know it is confessing the inner peace and beauty of God's Spirit within me that has caused even outward attractiveness, and I just give God the praise and glory! God's ways are so good!

Prayer

"Father God, thank You for making me who I am. Help me to accept and love myself unconditionally because that is how You love me.

"Please reveal Your love to me, that I will truly know, deep in my spirit, Your love for me. Then help my mind to comprehend this perfect love and realize who I am in Christ.

"In His loving Name, Amen."

7

FREEDOM IN THE HOLY SPIRIT

Receiving the Spirit

"If you love me, you will obey what I command. And I will ask the Father, and he will give you another Counselor to be with you forever — the Spirit of truth."

John 14:15-17

"But when he, the Spirit of truth, comes, he will guide you into all truth."

John 16:13

As a child I accepted Jesus as my Savior. However, until I was about thirty-five years old, Jesus was not truly Lord in my life, and I had not prayed to receive the Holy Spirit.

As the result of urgings by my youngest brother, in the winter of 1970-71 I went to hear a sermon about the Holy Spirit. At the close of that sermon I knelt and asked the Father to fill me with His Holy Spirit. I yielded my entire self to God.

The Holy Spirit did come into my life. I know it happened because the fruit of the Spirit, especially peace, began to be manifested in my life. God's Word became a delight to read instead of a chore, and joy became a reality in my everyday life.

Galations 5:22-23 lists the fruit of the Spirit as love, joy, peace, patience, kindness, goodness, faithfulness, gentleness and self-control. Not all of these were instantly obvious in my life! Remember, they are *fruit*. When we plant an apple tree or a peach tree we do not expect it to produce mature, ripened fruit in just a few days. We know that it takes some years for a fruit tree to develop to its mature potential and produce fruit.

We also know that a fruit tree needs care, watering, fertilizing and some pruning before bountiful fruit crops can be expected.

Therefore, we shouldn't expect the matured fruit of the Spirit to instantly appear in the Spirit-filled Christian's life. We need to be patient and willing to help, not being critical of him, because he will need time to mature, time for cultivation. Even after several years, I can see fruit that has not fully matured in me. I am still cultivating it and working toward the goal of *being rooted and established in love* (Eph. 3:17).

Christ's instructions to His disciples, after His resurrection and before He was taken into heaven, was that they wait in Jerusalem until they received the promised gift, the Holy Spirit. (Acts 1:4-5.)

In John 3:5, Christ instructed Nicodemus, *"...unless a man is born of water and the Spirit, he cannot enter the kingdom of God."*

The Holy Spirit came upon Jesus when He was baptized by John the Baptist. Luke 3:22 says that the Holy Spirit descended upon Him like a dove. Luke records that Christ was full of the Holy Spirit when He returned from the Jordan River (Luke 4:1.), and that He *returned to Galilee in the power of the Spirit* (Luke 4:14).

Christ is our example. Certainly if He needed the baptism and the empowering of the Holy Spirit, we also, as His followers, need the Holy Spirit for guidance and power in our lives.

In Luke 11:9-12 Jesus gives us instructions on how to receive the Holy Spirit: *"So I say to you: Ask and it will be given to you; seek and you will find; knock and the door will be opened to you"* (v. 9).

He goes on to say that if we, as earthly parents, know how to give our children good gifts, *"how much more will* (our) *Father in heaven give the Holy Spirit to those who ask him!"* (v. 13).

So when we ask God the Father, in Jesus' Name, for the Holy Spirit in our life, God's Word says that we will receive Him.

Here is a sample prayer for you to pray to receive the Holy Spirit in your life:

"Lord, I come to You in the Name of Jesus Christ, Your Son. I ask that You give me Your Holy Spirit in my life. My desire is that the Holy Spirit dwell within me, giving me power to live victoriously for You. I yield myself entirely to Your will, to be used in Your kingdom.

"Thank You for giving me Your Holy Spirit. I accept this gift from You right now. Amen."

If you prayed this prayer with a sincere heart, you can now know, by faith, that you are filled with the Spirit. God's Word says so!

The Fruit of the Spirit

The fruit of the Spirit is listed in Galations 5:22-23 and are as follows: *love, joy, peace, patience, kindness, goodness, faithfulness, gentleness and self-control.*

You can bring these into maturity in your life by what you confess.

Affirm Love

Need more love? Affirm:

Jesus' love is within me so that I have a loving, forgiving attitude toward everyone.

"All men will know that you are my disciples if you love one another" (John 13:35).

...let us not love [merely] in theory or in speech but in deed and in truth — in practice and in sincerity (1 John 3:18 *AMP*).

Whoever loves his brother lives in the light, and there is nothing in him to make him stumble (1 John 2:10).

So much has been written about love that I am not going to elaborate on it here. One thing you do need to know is that love can start by an act of your will and be strengthened by your words and actions. Speak love whether you feel it or not. Act in a loving way even if you don't really want to. When your words and your actions line up with God's ways concerning love, you will soon begin to *feel* love, too.

Affirm Joy

The second fruit listed is joy. If you have been a person who has been prone to depression or a negative outlook on life, you might feel that saying, "I have the joy of the Lord in my life," is a lie. But remember, Romans 4:17 says that God *calls things that are not as though they were,* and in faith you can do the same. It is not a lie. It is an agreement with the truth, God's Word, which says of God's redeemed: *...everlasting joy will crown their heads. Gladness and joy will overtake them* (Is. 51:11).

...you believe in him (Christ) *and are filled with an inexpressible and glorious joy, for you are receiving the goal of your faith, the salvation of your souls* (1 Peter 1:8-9).

Light is shed upon the righteous and joy on the upright heart (Ps. 97:11).

Affirm Peace

Another fruit of the Spirit is peace. If you have difficulty being calm, content and peaceful, you are certainly not alone. The large quantities of tranquilizers sold are evidence of that fact. But in Philippians 4:6 we are told: *Do not be anxious about anything.* Most worldly people would say that this is impossible, but we are to agree with God's Word and not man's reasonings.

Therefore, we can affirm:

I am at peace because Christ is within me.

...the mind controlled by the Spirit is life and peace (Rom. 8:6).

And the peace of God, which transcends all understanding, will guard your hearts and your minds in Christ Jesus (Phil. 4:7).

"Peace I leave with you; my peace I give you. I do not give to you as the world gives. Do not let your hearts be troubled and do not be afraid" (John 14:27).

I will listen to what God the Lord will say; he promises peace to his people (Ps. 85:8).

For he himself (Christ) *is our peace* (Eph. 2:14).

(The affirmations for the fruit for self-control are covered in Chapter 8, and the other fruits can be found on the affirmation cards along with scriptures to confess with them.)

The Gifts of the Spirit

Another thing that we are to seek are the gifts of the Spirit. First Corinthians 14:1 says: *Follow the way of love and eagerly desire spiritual gifts.*

These gifts are listed in 1 Corinthians 12. They include wisdom, knowledge, faith, healing, miraculous powers, prophecy, discernment of spirits, ability to speak in tongues and ability to interpret tongues.

Now I am going to tell some things here that may step on some "theological toes" on both sides of the Christian camp. But I am not as interested in not offending church leaders as I am desirous to see God's children free from doctrinal bondage!

Most of us have heard arguments for and against the gifts of the Spirit with the gift of tongues being the most often discussed. I will relate my experience at this point because I feel it will be helpful to many who, as I, have attended or still do attend churches who ignore or even preach against tongues.

When I asked for the Holy Spirit to fill me in 1970, I didn't even consider asking for His gifts so I did not speak in tongues. Yet I knew, and still know, that the Holy Spirit did come into my life at that point. It was not until 1979 that I began to lose my negative feelings about the gift of tongues. I realized the gift of tongues was not something God gave to people just to convince them He had come into them.

In her book, *The Healing Gifts of the Spirit*,[5] Agnes

---

[5]Trumpet Books, A.J. Holman Co., Philadelphia and New York, 1976

Sanford writes about her experiences in the Holy Spirit in a very low-key, logical manner. Our pastor patiently answered my many questions about this gift of speaking in tongues. An intercessor for our ministry received the gift of praying in tongues one day without even asking for it! In fact, at that point she didn't even *want* to pray in tongues because her church taught against it, but God was very explicit with her that if she wanted to continue in His blessings, she must be open to His Spirit's gifts.

As a result of these and other experiences, I finally arrived at the point, early in 1979, that I prayed, "Father, whatever gift You know that I need for our ministry or for myself, I am open to receive." (Secretly I was hoping for a gift or gifts other that prophecy or tongues.)

Praise the Lord! He is wiser that I am! Later that same evening, after the pastor and Derin had prayed for me, I had these "strange words" come across my mind and the next morning, very quietly, I began to pray in tongues during my private devotions.

No desperate begging, no big emotional high, just a quiet acceptance of the Holy Spirit praying to the Father through me, from the depths of my spirit.

I have since received other gifts from the Spirit such as prophecy, faith, and discerning of spirits, but tongues is the one I use most and would never want to be without.

And I have good news for you! The people who speak in tongues will be in heaven, and the people who do not speak in tongues will be there, too! And I am sure God is pleased that we are all walking in love with one another here on His footstool!

In praying with Christians desiring the gift of tongues, I have found that many from fundamentalist churches have difficulty receiving this gift. This is not because God hasn't given them His Spirit when they asked, but rather because (as a result of negative teaching in the past) they have a mental block that keeps the new language in their spirit from flowing freely and being expressed verbally. If this is your situation, do not become discouraged. Continue to believe and confess that you are baptized in the Holy Spirit and His gifts are operating in your life.

You can confidently affirm:

I am filled with and baptized in the Holy Spirit and have the fruit and gifts of the Spirit in my life.

You have already been given the verses and affirmations on the fruit. Here are some verses about the gifts:

Now to each one the manifestation of the Spirit is given for the common good. ...there is given through the Spirit... wisdom... knowledge... faith... healing... miraculous powers... prophecy... the ability to distinguish between spirits... tongues, and... interpretation of tongues (1 Cor. 12:7-10).

God also testified to it by... gifts of the Holy Spirit distributed according to his will (Heb. 2:4).

For the promise (of the Holy Spirit) is to and for you and your children, and to and for all that are far away, [even] to as many as the Lord our God invites and bids come to Himself (Acts 2:39 AMP).

He who speaks in a [strange] tongue edifies and improves himself, ...he who prophesies... edifies and improves the church... (1 Cor. 14:4 AMP).

Not everyone receives all of the gifts, but everyone

who wants God's best in his life should be open to receive any or all of them. It is not our place or right to tell God, "I would like the gift of healing or wisdom, but I will not accept the gift of prophecy or tongues."

What if Mary had refused to accept everything that God wished to bestow on her through the Holy Spirit? As a virgin, knowing Jewish laws, she knew being pregnant before marriage could mean death. Still she accepted the gift of the Holy Spirit, conception of Jesus Christ within her, and because of her obedience she became the most honored of all women.

We can not know all that God wishes to do for us, and through us for others. To realize the plan He has for us we must be open to accept whatever gift or gifts He has for us.

In Hebrews 2:4 we read, *God also testified to it* (salvation) *by signs, wonders, and various miracles, and gifts of the Holy Spirit distributed according to his will.*

First Corinthians 12:11 says, *All these* (gifts) *are the work of one and the same Spirit, and he gives them to each man, **just as he determines.** *Verse seven says, *Now to each man the manifestation of the Spirit is given **for the common good.***

We are a part of Christ's body. He knows what gift or gifts we need manifested in our lives for the good of His body. Our prayer should be that God would give us the gifts He sees that are needed to build His kingdom through us.

I feel that for a church or body of believers to function most effectively, it should have all of the gifts manifested within its members.

The gifts of the Spirit have been an area of great controversy among Christians. It seems that Satan has not wanted Christ's Church to realize its full potential in this area. Today the prophecy in Joel 2:28-29 is coming to fullfillment and the Holy Spirit is being *poured out* on many people. We must be careful not to quench the Spirit (1 Thess. 5:19.), and thereby miss God's fullest blessing on our life!

I offer this verse to anyone who may doubt that it is God's will for him to have the Holy Spirit in his life: *The man without the Spirit does not accept the things that come from the Spirit of God, for they are foolishness to him, and he cannot understand them, because they are spiritually discerned* (1 Cor. 2:14).

Prayer

"Lord God, I praise You for the Holy Spirit! Thank You, Jesus, for going to heaven so He could be sent back to earth to dwell within me. Thank You that I am baptized in the Holy Spirit and have His fruit and His gifts in my life.

"Please help me to be open to everything the Holy Spirit desires to do in my life. Help me not to quench or grieve Him in any way, but to be completely yielded to Your Spirit in every area.

"In Jesus' Name, Amen."

8
FREEDOM UNDER GOD'S CONTROL

The Controlled Person

The area of self-control in one's life is often where the battle for victorious living is won or lost.

In this area, too, we can "call things that are not as though they were." (Rom. 4:17.)

Controlled Appetite

I have counseled some people who were compulsive eaters. I had really not had much exposure to this problem before and didn't realize the depth and magnitude of problems this compulsion caused in people's lives.

Instead of being judgmental of people who have weight problems, I have become sympathetic with them after hearing of their struggles and knowing the reasons, which often go back to childhood days, that they have the problem of overeating.

But whether the overweight problem is caused by hurts from childhood, lack of self-discipline or poor nutrition and eating habits, God has the answer. I suggest you use this prayer:

"Dear Lord, I repent of the sins of gluttony and overeating and ask Your forgiveness for them. I cast down Satan's hold in my body and I establish temperance and self-control. I affirm that my body is the temple of the Holy Spirit and is under His control.

"Father God, please go back in time and heal all the psychological and spiritual hurts that have caused me to have a tendency to overeat. Please heal any physical imbalances that would cause me to gain weight. Put my spirit, mind and body into perfect harmony and balance.

"I come against all negative and derogatory words I have spoken about myself, about having difficulty losing weight and how easy it is for me to gain. I cast down these words and pronounce them null and void. Satan can no longer use these words against me. From this day forward, 'I resolve that my mouth will not sin.' (Ps. 17:13.)

"Thank You, Lord, for forgiving me and setting me free from bondage! I will not live after the dictates of the flesh, but after the dictates of the Spirit, in accordance with Romans 8:1 *(AMP)*.

"In Jesus' powerful Name, Amen."

Use this affirmation:

Christ has control of my appetite and eating habits. I am a slender person. I don't eat more than my body needs. It is easy for me to lose weight. My body's metabolism works perfectly.

Confess these scriptures:

"It is written: 'Man does not live on bread alone, but on every word that comes from the mouth of God' " (Matt. 4:4).

For the kingdom of God is not a matter of eating and drinking, but of righteousness, peace and joy in the Holy Spirit (Rom. 14:17).

So whether you eat or drink or whatever you do, do it all for the glory of God (1 Cor. 10:31).

God has given us an appetite for food and stomachs to digest it. But that doesn't mean we should eat more than we need (1 Cor. 6:13 TLB).

"...do not set your heart on what you will eat or drink; do not worry about it" (Luke 12:29).

"Is not life more important than food?" (Matt. 6:25).

In January Ellen decided she wanted to lose weight. She prayed, asking God to help her. Then, using the affirmations, she started to diet. In the next seven months she lost 60 pounds. In July she was chosen as one of the finalists in the Miss Teen Pageant in state competition.

She did not use any special diet. She cut down on her eating and prayed, "God, You know how much my body needs every day, so I just trust You to show me how much." Then she walked in obedience and used God's Word to overcome the overeating habit and to establish temperance and self-control in her life.

Ellen looks great and is delighted with the results of giving God control in her life!

Controlled Emotions

If you are a person who gets angry easily, here is a good affirmation for you:

My emotions are under the control of the Holy Spirit. I am patient and kind.

A patient man has great understanding, but a quick-tempered man displays folly (Prov. 14:29).

Whatever happens, conduct yourselves in a manner worthy of the gospel of Christ (Phil. 1:27).

Everyone should be quick to listen, slow to speak and

slow to become angry, for man's anger does not bring about the righteous life that God desires (James 1:19-20).

Do not be quickly provoked in your spirit, for anger resides in the lap of fools (Eccl. 7:9).

"In your anger do not sin": Do not let the sun go down while you are still angry, and do not give the devil a foothold (Eph. 4:26-27).

I would like to relate what has happened in my life in this area. For many years I had known that anger and resentment were a problem to me. I would become very angry with my husband if he did not arrive home at the time I expected him. I was often too harsh in my punishment of our children — punishing them out of anger instead of love. Then I read Tim LaHaye's book, *Spirit Controlled Temperament.*[6] I took his directives to heart.

I confessed anger as sin. I asked God to forgive me and to help me break the habit of anger in my life. My husband was impressed at the change in me. One time, when he came home late, his comment was, "I forgot you wouldn't be mad."

It has been over ten years since the Lord helped me with my anger, and now my family is surprised if I get angry! What a beautiful release for them and for me. I have much more joy and peace in my life. You, too, can be released from anger and the hurts it causes! First, repent and ask God's forgiveness; and then renew your habit patterns in the Word to develop gentleness, patience and self-control.

The Controlled Tongue

The Bible declares that our mouths, tongues and

[6]Tyndale House Publishers, Wheaton, Illinois, 1966

lips are to be used to praise God and to declare His Word and will.

We are also to be very careful what our lips and tongue say. The unpardonable sin (blasphemy of the Holy Spirit) is committed with the mouth: ...*anyone who speaks against the Holy Spirit will not be forgiven, either in this age or in the age to come* (Matt. 12:32).

James 3:9-10 gives us a warning: *With the tongue we praise our Lord and Father, and with it we curse men, who have been made in God's likeness. Out of the same mouth come praise and cursing. My brothers, this should not be.* James 1:26 also warns: *If anyone considers himself religious and yet does not keep a tight rein on his tongue, he deceives himself and his religion is worthless.*

Jesus said, *"But I tell you that men will have to give account on the day of judgment for every careless word they have spoken"* (Matt. 12:36).

If that last verse doesn't sober you — judgment day may seem far away and remote to you — then consider this: **In our life, this very day, we receive what we say with our mouth!**

Listen to yourself and to the people around you. You will be amazed at how much of what is said is negative. Those who are sick tell others about it; they repeat what the doctor says about the seriousness of their disease. You know people who seem to enjoy telling others about their health problems, and guess what? They have plenty of illness to talk about.

I have an easy time expecting health for our family. When someone isn't feeling well, we say, "Oh, you'll be better soon," or, "You'll feel fine by morning." In twenty-five years of marriage and with three children ages 22, 19, and 16, no one in our family has ever had to be in the hospital because of illness. Praise the Lord!

However, over the years we have not always been positive in our talk about money and we have had some financial problems that really puzzled us. Now we know our negative statements about our money, and our telling friends (with our mouths) about all the bad things that were happening to us financially kept us in financial bondage.

We have now realized our mistake and are working to renew our minds by stating that God's favor is on our finances. We are confessing His Word in this area and are seeing positive, even miraculous, results.

There are times when God does heal sickness and poverty instantaneously. That is a miracle, an act of God. However, what we are striving to learn are the ways of God. His ways usually follow natural laws and often He allows us to learn more about Him, as He, over a period of time, is healing our body or our financial circumstance.

I freely admit that there are still many situations in which I do not fully understand God's timing or His way of working things out. I *do* feel that the sooner we, His children, have mass belief, instead of mass unbelief, the more instant miracles we will see.

It is interesting to note how Satan has deceived us into using negative words and sayings as a part of our everyday speech. Consider a few with me.

What does death have to do with happiness? Yet people say that they are "thrilled to death" and "tickled to death" over things they're happy about.

The Bible says, *Do not be anxious about anything* (Phil. 4:6). Yet we say, "I'm anxious to see you." We really mean, "I'm looking forward with joy to seeing you."

Satan also has some "proverbs," sayings people commonly use that are outright lies!

For instance: "What you don't know won't hurt you." God says in His Word, *My people are destroyed from lack of knowledge"* (Hos. 4:6). Another lie is, "Sticks and stones may break my bones, but words will never hurt me." Proverbs 12:18 says: *Reckless words pierce like a sword, but the tongue of the wise brings healing.*

I have started really being aware of all my speech, even cliches and slang, because I know words are so powerful!

Say What You Want

A book which deals with saying what we want is, *What You Say is What You Get* by Don Gossett.[7] You may wish to read it. Watch your words to be sure they are positive and you will see positive results.

In Psalm 19:14 David wrote: *May the words of my mouth and the meditation of my heart be pleasing in your sight, O Lord, my Rock and my Redeemer.* This is a good verse to use in your prayers each morning.

I used to read Luke 17:5-6 and think my faith was too small: *The apostles said to the Lord, "Increase our faith!" He replied, "If you have faith as small as a mustard seed, you can say to this mulberry tree, 'Be uprooted and planted in the sea,' and it will obey you."*

Then one day when I read that scripture, a new thought came to me. I think Jesus was really saying,

[7]Whitaker House, Springdale, Pennsylvania, 1976

"Don't worry about how much faith you have: even if it is infinitesmal, act on it! Speak, say with your mouth what you want to see accomplished, and it will be."

Of course, Jesus knew that when the disciples did act on and state their faith, they would see results, which in turn would increase their faith.

Your affirmation should be:

My tongue is controlled by Christ, because His love is in me.

Do not let any unwholesome talk come out of your mouths, but only what is helpful for building others up... (Eph. 4:29).

Let your conversation be always full of grace, seasoned with salt, so that you may know how to answer everyone (Col. 4:6).

I have resolved that my mouth will not sin (Ps. 17:3).

James 3:8 says, *...but no man can tame the tongue.* But verse two of that same chapter says, *If anyone is never at fault in what he says, he is a perfect man, able to keep his whole body in check.* Is James contradicting himself? No. We must give God control of our tongue and let Him control our words, because man can not do it by himself!

Controlling Lust

The Bible says, *Flee from sexual immorality... he who sins sexually sins against his own body* (1 Cor. 6:18). This is not easy to do when the magazines, books, television shows and advertisers are seeking to appeal to the sensual desires of people.

To live victoriously we must learn to resist evil

effectively, especially in this area. The sex drive is a normal, natural drive and only wrong when we allow Satan to use it to cause us to lust.

We must eliminate pornographic literature and movies from our minds and lives, and concentrate on thoughts that are pure. ...*whatever is true, whatever is noble, whatever is right, whatever is pure, whatever is lovely, whatever is admirable — if anything is excellent or praiseworthy — think about such things* (Phil 4:8).

Lust is not an easy habit to break away from, but God promises in 1 Corinthians 10:13: *No temptation has seized you except what is common to man. And God is faithful; he will not let you be tempted beyond what you can bear. But when you are tempted, he will also provide a way out so that you can stand up under it.*

Some time ago I had a new insight on this verse. I used to wonder, and at times be angry at God, when I succumbed to temptation. I felt God had allowed me to be tempted "beyond what I could bear." I did not realize what the next part of the verse was saying. It says, "He will also provide a way out."

I found this "way out" was using the scriptures to resist Satan during times of temptation. When Jesus was tempted, He quoted God's Word. When we are tempted we can "stand up under it" by quoting God's Word. Don't argue with Satan on the mind level. Defeat him on the spiritual level. He knows God's Word is true and he does not like to hear it. Resist the devil with God's Word and he will flee and you will overcome temptation!

This is what to affirm:
I have the purity of Christ within me.

71

"Blessed are the pure in heart, for they shall see God" (Matt. 5:8).

Jesus Christ... gave himself for us to redeem us from all wickedness and to purify for himself a people that are his very own, eager to do what is good (Titus 2:13-14).

Since we have these promises, dear friends, let us purify ourselves from everything that contaminates body and spirit (2 Cor. 7:1).

And this is my prayer:... that you may be able to discern what is best and may be pure and blameless until the day of Christ (Phil. 1:9-10).

For the grace of God that brings salvation has appeared to all men. It teaches us to say "No" to ungodliness and worldly passions, and to live self-controlled, upright and godly lives in this present age (Titus 2:11-12).

A Controlled Spirit

One day I realized that in my "control" affirmations there were really none that spoke about my spirit being controlled by God, so I wrote this affirmation:

As an act of my will I place my spirit under the control of God's Holy Spirit. My spirit is subject to God's Spirit and is obedient to His will.

Some of the verses I found to confess are:

...live not after the dictates of the flesh, but after the dictates of the Spirit (Rom. 8:1 AMP).

...those who live in accordance with the Spirit have their minds set on what the Spirit desires. ...the mind controlled by the Spirit is life and peace (Rom. 8:5-6).

...live by the Spirit, and you will not gratify the desires of the sinful nature (Gal. 5:16).

Along with the control of your spirit, give God

control of your mind also. Affirm:

I have the mind of Christ and my thoughts and attitudes are obedient to the Holy Spirit.

Verses to confess:

...take captive every thought to make it obedient to Christ (2 Cor. 10:5).

...let your minds be remade and your whole nature thus transformed (Rom. 12:2 *The New English Bible*).

...we have the mind of Christ (1 Cor. 2:16).

Do the things I've suggested in this chapter and the verses in Ephesians 4:22-24 will come true in your life: *You were taught, with regard to your former way of life, to put off your old self ...to be made new in the attitude of your minds; and to put on the new self, created to be like God in true righteousness and holiness.*

Prayer

"Dear Lord, I want you to control my life completely. So as an act of my will, I place my spirit, heart, mind and body in Your hand.

"I cast down any rebellion against You or Your ways. I come against any and all strongholds Satan has had in my life and say that Satan no longer has any power over me.

"I ask You, God, to establish righteousness in every area of my life. Thank You for giving me a spirit of obedience and self-control. I will walk in Your ways.

"In Jesus' Name, Amen."

9

FREEDOM IN YOUR FAMILY

Family Wholeness

You will find that the positive confessions in the preceding chapters will also benefit your relationships in your family. They will see the growth in your life and will begin to respond favorably to the positive change in you.

(If you are an unmarried or childless person, please don't omit the reading of this chapter. The ideas presented will work in other relationships too. Also, you may be able to help someone who is having family troubles by relating these concepts to them.)

Today's families seem to be literally falling apart. We see more and more divorces, child abuse, teenage suicides, juvenile crime and runaways. The educators, sociologists, and psychiatrists look desperately for solutions, but find none that are lasting. The answers cannot be found outside of God and His Word. We need to "know the Scriptures" about family relationships. The Bible has many directives in this area.

(For a few years, I contemplated writing a book about raising children, so I have plenty of material on the subject which I could present here. I'll refrain from that, however, and suggest that if you would like further ideas about how to bring up your children you send for my tape entitled, "Raising Children in God's Ways," tape 2 of the "Marriage and Family" series.)

Beth came to me because she felt she didn't love her child, Janice, as she should. In fact, Satan had convinced Beth that she didn't love Janice at all.

Often when I'm counseling with a person I can see past what he is saying with words and perceive what his heart or spirit is *really* saying. This was true in Beth's case.

Her mouth said, "I don't love Janice and I've even considered giving her away so she can be raised in love not anger."

I heard her spirit, her true self, saying, "I really love Janice but my own feelings of being rejected are causing me to react in anger toward her."

I shared with Beth that she really did love Janice, but she wasn't convinced. However, being a good student, she did take the affirmations and Bible verses I gave her home with her and began to say them each day. Things slowly improved, but Satan wasn't ready to give up his stronghold on that family yet.

Janice started doing naughty and exasperating things on a regular basis. Beth reacted with anger and severe punishment. Beth was very upset and regretful. Again I saw past Satan's smoke screen to Beth's true heart of love for all children, including Janice.

This time I prayed a creative prayer and asked for a miracle from God, and He did it! Driving home from my house Beth suddenly became aware that God was love and He was in her. She then recalled the scriptural affirmation: *Greater is he that is in you, than he that is in the world* (1 John 4:4 *KJV*). She realized that God's love in her was stronger that Satan's hate, and she then realized that she truly did love Janice.

About three days later I had occasion to be with

Beth and Janice. Janice looked at Beth and said, "I love you, Mom!"

"I love you, too," replied Beth.

Janice looked at me with a radiant smile and exclaimed, "She always says that!"

God's Ways For Your Children

Our children reflect back in their actions and attitudes what we say to and about them. Be careful not to "curse" them with phrases like: "You're just like (name of a problem relative)!"; "You'll never amount to anything!"; "You are so lazy!"; "You'll never learn, will you?"; etc. Instead, bless them with positive phrases: "I like the way you set the table"; "You are developing mature judgment — that's a good idea"; "I'm thankful you're our daughter (or son)"; "You are learning to be responsible"; etc.

Be careful also to treat them with respect and common courtesy. Say please when you ask them to do something and remember to thank them when the job is done! Don't call them to you only when you have work you want them to do. Call sometimes just to share something positive — a flower, a butterfly, a beautiful sunset, a compliment, or maybe a freshly-baked cookie. The results will be a better answering service!

Here is an affirmation and some scriptures to use:

I have God's wisdom and compassion in my relationship with my children (or child's name).

...teach the young women ...to love their children (Titus 2:4 *KJV*).

Our children too shall serve him for they shall hear from

us about the wonders of the Lord (Ps. 22:30 *TLB*).

"All your sons will be taught by the Lord, and great will be your children's peace" (Is. 54:13).

...do not exasperate your children; instead, bring them up in the training and instruction of the Lord (Eph. 6:4).

A key to raising stable children in today's unstable society is to have a Christ-like spirit that carries over into everyday life in the home. Parents who profess Christ, attend church, act religious when around other Christians, but do not live Christ-like lives in their own families, leave an open opportunity for Satan to get to their children through doubt and resentment. These children from "Christian" homes often have a harder time serving Christ in their lives that those from completely non-Christian homes.

Your affirmations on self-control will help you be consistent in this area. Some further verses to ponder are:

I will try to walk a blameless path, but how I need your help, especially in my own home, where I long to act as I should (Ps. 101:2 *TLB*).

The fool who provokes his family to anger and resentment will finally have nothing worthwhile left (Prov. 11:29 *TLB*).

In Titus 2:4-6 older women of the church are instructed to help train the younger women to love their husbands and children, to be self-controlled and pure, to be busy at home and to be kind.

How our society today needs this kind of mother! One who sees her *first responsibility* as that of providing a secure, loving home for her family. Many of the people we counsel are from homes where parents did not follow Biblical principles in raising their children.

Too many mothers are so busy at jobs, clubs and even church activities or a ministry they feel God has given them, that the home is neglected. Some who are home are not busy in the right ways — they are too busy watching television, especially soap operas. Self-control may involve turning the television off and cleaning the house!

If we, as mothers, do not practice purity in our lives we cannot expect our children to avoid sexual impurity in our sex-oriented society. (In Chapter 8 there is a section on purity.)

Our children often meet unkindness from teachers or peers. They need a haven of love and kindness in their home.

There are many books about child rearing that are written from the worldly point of view. They have lots of unproven ideas about how to raise well-adjusted children. Don't follow their advice unless it is in line with what the Bible says, especially in the area of discipline. When my children were young a popular ''child expert'' advised against spanking, then in later years he changed his mind and said that advice had been wrong. (Fortunately, I had not taken his advice in the first place.)

The Bible says, *Folly is bound up in the heart of a child, but the rod of discipline will drive it far from him* (Prov. 22:15).

Proverbs 29:15 states: *The rod of correction imparts wisdom, but a child left to itself disgraces his mother.*

In reading Hebrews 12, we find that the writer assumed that everyone had been disciplined by his father and respected him for it, and because of that discipline knew how to submit to God's correction. The home situation in those days must have been quite different from today's!

If we discipline correctly, the Bible has some promises for us.

Train a child in the way he should go, and when he is old he will not turn from it (Prov. 22:6).

Discipline your son, and he will give you peace; he will bring delight to your soul (Prov. 29:17).

One word of warning. Do not discipline, especially using physical punishment, in anger. I know this is difficult, but our object, as Christian parents, is that of helping our children grow in good judgment and self-control. When we lose our self-contol and punish in anger, it is easy to see why that goal is not met, because our children get confusing signals.

I'm sorry I didn't realize the importance of this truth when my children were toddlers. I still sometimes get angry at their behavior, but now I give myself a cooling-off period, telling them I will decide on their punishment later when I'm over being angry.

If you have sometimes punished in anger (and who hasn't?), don't be afraid to ask your child's forgiveness. Not for the punishment, if it was deserved, but for punishing them in anger. Children understand that parents are human and they don't expect us to be perfect. I've found that my children are very ready to forgive me in this area.

Always ask forgiveness as soon as you can, and especially before your children go to bed at night. Anger that is left to turn into resentment leads to bitterness that can affect a relationship for years.

Lately there has been some teaching in church

circles that really emphasizes "using the rod," spanking children with a wooden spoon or some other such object. I agree with the use of a "tool" rather than the hand, but I have felt a caution in my spirit against this "pat answer" to all discipline problems.

I spanked my children when they were small but I also used other kinds of punishment, such as sitting them on a chair or sending them to their room. We need to seek the wisdom of God in the area of discipline, making sure it is based on love and good judgment rather than a currently popular "religious idea."

I know of one small boy who was severely spanked in a church children's group and it did much damage to his spirit, causing his parents to have problems with rebellious behavior for quite a while. I feel this kind of discipline should definitely be left to parents.

The other teaching that has really troubled my spirit is the spanking of teenagers. I cannot quote a specific scripture that states, "Do not spank your teenaged child," so I will just present my viewpoint and allow you to draw your own conclusions.

My first reason for opposing the spanking of teenagers is based on common sense. Often a teenager is larger and in better physical condition than the parent. If he should decide that he is not going to allow himself to be spanked, then the parent may very well have a difficult time getting it done.

On the other hand, if the teenager is cooperative enough to allow himself to be spanked, I would question whether he really deserved or needed a spanking in the first place.

Then in reading and pondering the scriptures

about the "rod" being used for discipline, I noticed that the writers kept referring to the "child." In the Jewish tradition, an offspring was considered a child up to the day of his thirteenth birthday, at which time a *bar mizvah* ceremony was held to indicate that the boy was now considered a man and therefore no longer under his parents' supervision. From that time on he was considered to be responsible for himself in regard to the law and commandments.

Therefore I feel that the scriptures on disciplining a "child" might not apply to youngsters past the age of thirteen. Other ways of discipline were probably used if needed.

As I have stated, this is my own opinion. Ask God to reveal to you His wisdom in regard to you and your own family situation.

He who fears the Lord has a secure fortress, and for his children it will be a refuge (Prov. 14:26).

In today's society our children certainly do need a refuge and a fortress provided for them in our homes. It is up to us as their parents to provide this security.

My children have been quite open in sharing with me about the drug problems and the sexual views they encounter in the public schools. I have been appalled at the kind of filthy language and actions to which they are subjected. They also have so many friends from broken homes that I expect they cannot help but wonder if there is a possibility that their father and I might one day divorce.

Another thing that has concerned me is the emphasis on the occult which has developed lately in movies, on television and in literature. Rock singers and musical groups use it as an attention getter. As

Christians we must be aware that any contact with the occult is to be avoided completely. (This includes seances, ouija boards and even horoscopes.)

Let no one be found among you who... practices divination or sorcery, interprets omens, engages in witch-craft, or casts spells, or who is a medium or spiritist or who consults the dead. Anyone who does these things is detestable to the Lord...

Deuteronomy 18:10-12

We need to be aware of all these avenues that Satan is using to try to draw our children away from God's ways. We can combat them by being aware of them and being open so our children are free to talk to us about everything; by taking a firm stand on what is right and wrong, from the Bible's teachings; and, most importantly of all, by being an example that is so attractive that our children will be drawn to Christ and His love. Here is a prayer you can pray to help establish a right relationship with your children:

"Father, I come to You in the Name of Jesus, Your Son and my Savior. I ask Your forgiveness for my wrong attitudes of anger, unforgiveness and hostility toward my children. Also forgive me, Father, for the unkind and harsh words I've spoken to or about them. I repent of any unfair punishment I've used in disciplining them. Thank You, Father, for forgiving me and I accept Your mercy.

"I now, as an act of my will, allow forgiveness to flow through Jesus and then through me to _____. I forgive and release him/her right now for any hurt,

shame or worry that he/she has caused me.

"I accept _____ as a child, given by You, in Your infinite wisdom, to me.

"I now rebuke and cancel all negative statements I've ever make about _____ in the past, and I come against those statements with the energy of Jesus' blood to nullify any negative influence they might have over _____ or myself or our family situation.

"Help me to see _____ with Your eyes of love, to see his/her uniqueness and potential in the same way as You view them. I make a decision of my will to accept and love _____ and to treat him/her with compassion and understanding from this time forward.

"I bless _____ with a spirit of cooperation. I bless him/her with self-confidence and peace.

"I ask, Father, that You, through the healing power of Jesus Christ, heal the past hurt and anger that we have had in our relationship.

"I say that we are now free to develop a new relationship based on love and compassion, understanding and cooperation. Thank You, Lord!

"In Jesus' Name, Amen."

Love Your Spouse

It has been said that it is more important for children to know that their parents love each other than that they love them. This is because of the deep need that each person has for security. Today's society and the world situation certainly doesn't provide much security. A Christ-centered home can and should.

Just being a Christian doesn't automatically assure that we love our spouse, as many who read this book could confirm, nor does it guarantee compatibility in marriage. Satan has tricked us into making negative confessions in our marriages and then we reap the attendant problems. If you have been making statements similar to these — "My husband never remembers special days"; "He's hurt me so many times I just can't forgive him again"; "He never really listens to me"; "My wife is a lousy cook — she can ruin a T.V. dinner"; "The house is a mess, I don't know what she does all day"; "All she does is nag, nag, nag"; "She is never ready on time, I don't understand why she can't get organized" — then you need to change your confessions. You are "cursing" your mate and you will continue to get what you say.

Start now to bless your husband or wife and refuse to perpetuate their mistakes by talking about them.

For the Wife

Make this affirmation:

I submit myself to _____ as to the Lord. He
(husband's name)

is my head and loves me as Christ loves the Church.

Wives, submit to your husbands, as is fitting in the Lord (Col. 3:18).

A wife of noble character who can find?... Her husband has full confidence in her... and he praises her (Prov. 31:10, 11, 28).

He has taken me to the banquet hall, and his banner over me is love (Song of Songs 2:4).

It is interesting to note, as we counsel people, the difference between the weaknesses of men and women.

(I'm going to discuss the wife's problems first — but don't get too happy, husband, your turn is coming.)

As a wife, you need to especially guard against these "besetting sins":

Gossip: Do not go from person to person seeking a sympathetic ear as you tell your husband's faults. If you truly need counsel, find one Word-founded friend (or perhaps your pastor) and tell her (or him) the situation. Then find Biblical solutions and start confessing what God wants for your husband and marriage.

Manipulation: This one is sneaky. If you are not sure whether you are guilty of it or not, ask your husband, children and your closest friend. People know when they are being manipulated — even if it is the "sweetest little lady in the world" who is doing it.

A beautiful young woman came to counsel with me and I was very puzzled when she said her husband had almost zero interest in their sexual relationship.

After getting to know her and her husband well I discovered that this sweet, beautiful wife was undoubtedly the most skilled manipulator I'd ever seen. I soon figured out the cause of their problem. In the one place where she couldn't make him perform — he didn't!

Satan manipulates, trying to get people to do things against their will. Refuse to be like him in any way!

Instead of gossiping and manipulating, release your husband and his faults to God and let God change him. You can aid in the process by praying correctly. For example:

Bless your husband with a thirst for righteousness; with a desire to read God's Word; with the fruits of the Spirit of love, joy, peace, patience, etc; and praise the Lord that he is the spiritual leader in your home.

Bless him with wisdom and consideration toward the children and with good stewardship and wisdom in financial dealings. Also bless him with a spirit of purity and with self-control. Then get prepared to see wonderful changes as you make these affirmations:

I love _____. He is my provider and security. I support his decisions.

...train the younger women to love their husbands... and to be subject to their husbands, so that no one will malign the word of God (Titus 2:4-5).

...the wife must respect her husband (Eph. 5:33).

The wise woman builds her house, but with her own hands the foolish one tears hers down (Prov. 14:1).

For the Husband

In God's Word husbands are commanded to love their wives as Christ loved the Church. (Eph. 5:25.)

Most often, the way that Satan tries to destroy this love relationship is through *selfishness.* Many men seem to be very prone to do what they want to do regardless of the family's needs or desires. This tendency shows up in two areas, time and money.

A recent study reported that statistics show that in the United States today most fathers spend less than

e minutes of quality time per day with their children.
Vhy? Because of selfishness! Most fathers would
rather watch television than spend a half-hour playing
a game with or reading to their children.

A very common complaint that I hear from the
wives I counsel is that there is no communication with
their husbands because he spends the entire evening
watching television, reading the newspaper or
magazines or books, or even staying on the phone
much of the evening on business calls. The husband
who buries himself in other activities makes his wife
feel unwanted and neglected.

Selfishness also enters into the money situation
in many families. How many husbands have bought
what they personally desired (golf clubs, a new gun,
fishing equipment, or even a new car) while their
family was in need of basic clothing? Far too many have
taken this selfish route. Husband, you say that you
love your wife, but your actions cause her to have real
doubts. You are late to come home but don't bother
to call so she can adjust the dinner hour accordingly.
You spend money on hunting and fishing equipment
or new golf clubs while your wife and children shop
garage sales for clothes. Even though your wife works
at a job outside the home just as many hours a day
as you do, yet you refuse to help her do the chores
around the house like cleaning or washing dishes
because (according to you) that is ''woman's work.''
You almost always insist on having things your way.
You give your wife the ''silent treatment'' when you
are angry.

All of these are indications of selfishness, the ''me
first'' attitude. If this describes you, then you need to

repent, ask God's forgiveness and change by making this affirmation:

I love my wife, _____. She is God's gift to me. She has my protection and support.

Husbands, love your wives, just as Christ loved the church... (Eph. 5:25).

...may you rejoice in the wife of your youth... may you ever be captivated by her love (Prov. 5:18-19).

Love... is patient and kind... it is not rude... love [God's love in us] does not insist on its own rights or its own way for it is not self-seeking... (1 Cor. 13:4-5 AMP).

"For this reason a man will leave his father and mother and be united to his wife, and the two will become one flesh" (Eph. 5:31).

Husbands, ...be considerate as you live with your wives, ...so that nothing will hinder your prayers (1 Pet. 3:7).

...a prudent wife is from the Lord (Prov. 19:14).

...a woman who fears the Lord is to be praised. Give her the reward she has earned... (Prov. 31:30-31).

Pride is the other area in which men often seem to fall into Satan's trap. Proverbs 16:5 states: *Everyone proud and arrogant in heart is disgusting, hateful and exceedingly offensive to the Lord (AMP).*

Self-sufficiency is a form of pride. Many men feel that they must be self-made successes, saying, "God helps those who help themselves." Pride puts self on the throne. Some go the "intellectual" route and others the "hard work" route, but both depend on their own skills instead of on God.

"Pride goes before a fall" has been quoted so often that some people don't realize it comes from the Bible, but it does. It is found in Proverbs 16:18. Pride also causes a person to be double-minded, and James 1:6-8 says that the double-minded person shouldn't expect to receive anything from the Lord. Your prayers aren't being answered? Check to see that you are humble before the Lord. If not, pray and ask God's forgiveness; humble yourself before Him and repent.

A patient man has great understanding (Prov. 14:29).

Be completely humble and gentle; be patient, bearing with one another in love (Eph. 4:2).

Love is patient, love is kind... It is not self-seeking, it is not easily angered, it keeps no record of wrongs (1 Cor. 13:4-5).

For Both of You

An excellent affirmation for both husbands and wives who have had hurts in their marriage (and who hasn't?) is the following:

I have forgiven completely all past mistakes and hurts in our marriage and have unconditional love in our relationship.

These scriptures will make that forgiveness permanent:

Bear with each other and forgive whatever grievances you may have against one another. Forgive as the Lord forgave you (Col 3:13).

Be kind and compassionate to one another, forgiving each other, just as in Christ God forgave you (Eph. 4:32).

"For if you forgive men when they sin against you, your heavenly Father will also forgive you" (Matt. 6:14).

Love forgets mistakes; nagging about them parts the best of friends (Prov. 17:9 *TLB*).

I watched a divorce take place that could have been avoided if this last scripture had been affirmed and then put into practice.

If you are still talking about something your husband or wife did several years ago that hurt you, you are not forgiving as the Lord forgave you. God forgives and forgets. As humans we do not have that divine ability to completely forget, but we can have the grace to keep from bringing up the situation again and again.

Many couples we have counseled have used these affirmations and seen positive results. Family members have shown more love toward each other. Husbands and wives have seen improvement in their communication, their sexual relationship and their understanding of each other.

Just recently I received a phone call from Leah. Less than a week earlier I had met and shared with her for about three hours. I explained how affirmations could work in her home to bring about some needed changes.

She was so excited when she called. She said, "I can't believe it! Here's what's happening." She went on to relate that her husband was taking two or three days off from work to take the family skiing. (Before this he had felt he was too busy to take any time off at all to spend with them.)

Also her sons were getting along much better since she had been blessing them with a spirit of cooperation and of love toward each other. One had actually offered, without being asked, to let the other ride his bike. (Before this time, Joe's bike had been strictly off-limits to his brother, who was not even allowed to touch it.)

Leah was also encouraged because the Holy Spirit had been bringing scripture verses to her mind that fit in with the affirmations. She was so encouraged and was praising God for the good things that were happening in her home.

God's Word is powerful. When we confess it and believe its power, we see results!

Prayer

"Father, I come to You in the Name of Jesus, Your Son. I ask forgiveness for the times I have been selfish, unforgiving, inconsiderate and hostile in my marriage.

(If you have been physically unfaithful in your marriage, ask forgiveness for that also)

"My actions of the past have wounded _____'s spirit and damaged the oneness of spirit that should be in our marriage. I repent of these acts and attitudes that have 'broken the faith' of our marriage, and I determine in my will to turn away from them.

"From now on I will seek Your wisdom in our marriage. I will show consideration, compassion, love, and forgiveness in our day-to-day relationship.

"Father, I am now ready to forgive _____ for everything that he/she has ever done to hurt me in any way. I ask for Your divine forgiveness to flow through Jesus and then through me to _____. I forgive him/her and release him/her right now.

"I rebuke and cancel all negative words I have ever said about _____ or our marriage. I say that they can no longer operate against us or our home in any way. I ask that You put a watch on my mouth that I will never again say negative things against _____ or our marriage.

"I now bless _____ with love, and light, and with spiritual growth. I bless our marriage with a spirit of love and forgiveness. I bless both of us, in Jesus' Name, with assurance that we are loved and accepted by each other. I ask that the spirit of our marriage be totally healed and that we become truly one in You.

"I ask that our marriage and home be a witness to this hurting world of what God can do to give true love and joy in human relationships.

"I praise and thank You for blessing us and for giving us fulfillment in our marriage and home.

"In Christ's Name, Amen."

(For further teachings on marriage, order my tape, "The Renewed Marriage," tape 1 of the "Marriage and Family" series.)

10

PHYSICAL FREEDOM

For years the Church spiritualized the Bible to the point where God's promises for physical blessings (health and prosperity) were hardly believed by the average Christian. You will find that many Christians today still do not accept that God desires His children to be healthy and prosperous.

God's Will Is Health

For a long time, contrary to all the arguments from "suffering saints," I felt it had to be God's will for us, His children, to be well! My common sense argued against illness being God's will.

As a parent, is it pleasing to you for your child to be sick or hurting? Not if you are a normal parent! We suffer when our children suffer and we sincerely want them to be healthy and strong. I'm even distressed when one of our pets is sick. Certainly God loves us more than we love our children or pets!

Our very inner being knows that we shouldn't be sick. If we really believe it is God's will for us to be ill we should not go to a doctor or take medication but just passively accept sickness and let "God's will be done." In fact, if God gets glory from our sickness, shouldn't we be praying to be sick so we can bring Him more glory? You can see how absurd the "God's will is illness" argument sounded to me.

Another question I had was, if it is God's will that we be sick, how come there is no illness in heaven where His perfect will is done? In the Lord's Prayer,

Jesus told us to pray, *Thy kingdom come, Thy will be done in earth, as it is in heaven* (Matt. 6:10 *KJV*). If God's will being done in heaven brought an absence of pain and suffering, why wasn't God's will the same here on earth? These were things I kept wondering about.

Therefore, I was delighted when I read this passage in *The Healing Power of the Bible* by Agnes Sanford:

"Indeed, we are sometimes so far away from this 'divine madness' that we encourage the devil by saying that illness is the will of God. We might as well say that plant lice and fungi are the will of the gardener, or that a house so poorly built that it cannot stand up straight is the will of the contractor.

*"Jesus never questioned whether or why He should heal. Nor did anyone ever say to Him, 'Why do you make men whole?' The reason was obvious: because God made men in His image and likeness and they were **supposed** to be whole.'"*[8]

Now let's look at the Word of God, the basis upon which every believing Christian should establish God's will. In the Old Testament we read in Deuteronomy 7:15 where Moses was pronouncing God's blessing upon His people. He tells them: *"The Lord will keep you free from every disease."*

In Exodus 23:25-26 God Himself declares: *"I will take away sickness from among you... I will give you a full life span."*

In the New Testament, Matthew writes: *"He* (Christ) *took up our infirmities and carried our diseases"*

[8]Trumpet Books, A.J. Holman Co., Philadelphia and New York, 1969, pp. 170-171

(Matt. 8:17). This is a quote from Isaiah 53:4 and *does* refer to physical healing because just preceding this verse in Matthew, Jesus had healed Peter's mother-in-law and "all the sick" brought to Him, which Matthew said was *to fulfill what was spoken through the prophet Isaiah* (v. 17).

Christ said He came to do the will of His Father. (John 6:38.) I cannot find even one incident where Jesus turned a sick person away saying, "It is not God's will for you to be well."

No, in the Gospels, which tell of many healings, we read that *he healed all their sick* (Matt. 12:15). We also see in the Gospels that when Jesus sent out His disciples to minister in His Name, one of the things He instructed them to do was, *"Heal the sick..."*(Matt. 10:8).

At this point the disbelievers usually bring up the Apostle Paul's "thorn in the flesh." Even if Paul's thorn was sickness (which cannot be proven scripturally), it was sent to keep him from being too ecstatic from the visions he had seen. (2 Cor. 12:7-10.) How many Christians do you know who are such visionaries that they need a thorn in their flesh? It's time that we pull Paul's festering thorn out of our disbelieving selves and let God heal us!

But when he asks, he must believe and not doubt, because he who doubts is like a wave of the sea, blown and tossed by the wind. That man should not think he will receive anything from the Lord (James 1:6-7).

Our doubts are killing us! Sickness is a result of sin and Satan. We should resist it, overcome it, and walk in divine health.

I make this confession even when I feel sick or am

in pain. (I'm not yet to the point where God's perfect will is always seen in my body.) I have found that it takes persistent, consistent confession of the Word on healing to overcome the years of false teaching concerning God's will and health.

Christ's light is in me completely healing my spirit, heart, mind and body.

...by his wounds you have been healed (1 Pet. 2:24).

"He took up our infirmities and carried our diseases" (Matt. 8:17).

He (God) *sent forth his word and healed them* (Ps. 107:20).

Oh Lord my God, I called to you for help and you healed me (Ps. 30:2).

My son,... listen closely to my words. ...keep them within your heart; for they are life to those who find them and health to a man's whole body (Prov. 4:20-22).

Then your light will break forth like the dawn, and your healing will quickly appear (Is. 58:8).

Do not be wise in your own eyes; fear the Lord and shun evil. This will bring health to your body... (Prov. 3:7-8).

And the prayer offered in faith will make the sick person well; the Lord will raise him up (James 5:15).

These confessions are definitely yielding fruit in my life. Since I started confessing health I have been healed of migraine headaches, of a cyst in my breast, various flu and cold type symptoms, and in general have been in much better health than in the past.

Common Questions

You may be asking yourself, "If all this is true, then why are so many Christians sick?" And you can give many examples. I probably cannot answer all your questions completely, but here are some thoughts for you to consider.

First, we cannot determine God's will for His children by observing what happens to other Christians, no matter how good or sincere they may seem to us. We cannot look at people, even Christian people, for a sure example of God's ways. The verses I've already quoted show that God's will is for His children to be in health.

Jesus said that He came to do the will of His Father. (John 6:38.) Look through the Gospels. Over and over they tell how Jesus healed people. Never did He say, "It is God's will that you be sick. He will receive glory from your suffering." Instead we are told that *Jesus went throughout Galilee, ...healing every disease and sickness among the people* (Matt. 4:23).

Another reason Christians are sick is because of unbelief; not always their own, but the general unbelief of their churches and friends. Read Mark 6:5-6 where we are told that Jesus could not do any miracles and healed only a few sick people in His own home town because of the lack of faith of the people there.

Many Christians do not treat their bodies as temples of the Holy Spirit. They overeat and eat the wrong kinds of foods. I read recently that 46% of Americans are overweight.

Without proper diet, exercise and rest we cannot expect our bodies to be completely healthy. When we neglect good health practices we are breaking natural laws, set up by God, and He very seldom violates these laws.

Talk to a medical doctor today and he will tell you

that a large percentage of illness is psychosomatic. It is the payment our physical bodies make for the unresolved fear, guilt, anger, and unforgiveness we allow to remain in our lives.

In 1 Corinthians 11:17-32, Paul writes to the people about taking Communion without first having examined themselves to make sure they were worthy. He said that this was why many of them were sick and some had even fallen asleep (died).

Therefore, we must cooperate with God and nature by having faith, good health practices, and a clear conscience before expecting good health. When our spirits are a "new creation" and our minds are renewed in God's Word, our bodies will benefit and receive healing.

My husband and I met a friend for breakfast. We had not seen this man for about a year. He came ready to argue with us about God's will concerning health and prosperity.

One of his statements that he seemed to think would settle the question was, "Well, everyone has to get sick and die!"

That very day during my daily devotional time I read this verse in Job: *You will come to the grave in full vigor, like sheaves gathered in season* (Job. 5:26).

We do not have to be sick to die; all that needs to take place is for our spirits to leave our bodies. If you carefully read about the Old Testament saints who followed God, you will find that they did not die of illness. Their deaths are reported in this way: *So Joseph died at the age of a hundred and ten* (Gen. 50:26); *Moses was a hundred and twenty years old when he died, yet his eyes were not weak nor his strength gone* (Deut. 34:7); *Then*

David rested with his fathers and was buried in the City of David (1 Kings 2:10).

Contrast this with the fate of Ahaziah, a king of Israel, who *did evil in the eyes of the Lord* (2 Chron. 22:4). He was informed by the prophet Elijah: *"Because you have done this* (consulted a false god), *you will never leave the bed you are lying on. You will certainly die!"* So he died, *according to the word of the Lord that Elijah had spoken* (2 Kings 1:16-17).

And, of course, there is Enoch — who didn't die at all! The Word says: *Enoch walked with God; then he was no more, because God took him away* (Gen. 5:24).

The next two stories are related as examples of what God desires to do for His children. Both of these ladies had prayer for healing of their hurting spirits with physical healing following.

Do not use these stories to "help" your faith. Faith comes by hearing God's Word. However, Christ's ministry was confirmed by healings and miracles and our ministry should bear similar fruit.

Healing From Arthritis
A good friend called me to chat for a while on the phone. In the course of the conversation she told me that she was having severe pain in her right hand and wrist. In fact, the pain was so severe that she had to have her husband help her bathe, as it was too painful for her to hold the soap or wash cloth.

I told her that I would pray for her healing. I said for her not to worry about having faith for this healing — I'd have the faith for her. At that point in time I didn't know her medical history, but she related these facts to me later.

In the summer of 1976, the doctor diagnosed that Sue had rheumatoid arthritis. She was having muscle spasms and aching in her joints. She was sent to a specialist who performed a bone scan which confirmed the diagnosis of rheumatoid arthritis.

Knowing Sue as well as I do, I know she is not the type person who gives in to pain unless it is really severe. Yet in the next year she was subject to pain day after day. She took many kinds of medication, but none of them helped.

Her hand became so stiff that, after holding an object for a while, she had trouble opening it again. Previously, Sue had been a very healthy person, usually not even having colds or flu. Now Satan laid fear on her as she observed the crippling effect arthritis had on the other patients in the doctor's waiting room.

A couple of days after I had prayed for Sue, she was much improved. Later I had opportunity to share with her about Christ's desire to heal her from hurtful childhood memories. She allowed my husband and me to pray for her. Sue then started affirming her healing and confessing the scriptures on healing that I had shared with her.

Gradually the arthritis symptoms have gone away. Recently Sue told me, ''I still sometimes have a minor symptom, but when I do I say, 'It is just a symptom because I've been healed!'''

Not only is Sue free of arthritis, she is free in her spirit also. She has a radiance and joy that can be seen by others. Her faith is strong in God's goodness because she sees many evidences of His healing in herself, her marriage, and her children.

Healing from Allergies and Depression

The phone rang late one afternoon. I did not know the young woman calling or the severity of her problem, but after we talked a short time she informed me that she was about to commit suicide. I assured her that I would be at her place within a half-hour.

Driving there in my car I thought, "What do I know about helping someone this near suicide?" But right away I asked God to supply wisdom and I confessed that I had the mind of Christ. (1 Cor. 2:16.)

Lisa had been suffering from severe allergies for six years. She was allergic to animals, perfumes, hair sprays and most foods. She had not eaten a normal meal for six years. Her diet was limited to 20 foods. However, Lisa was a very strong person and had been able to cope with the allergies quite well.

What had brought her to the point of suicide was the fact that, for the past few months, her mind had not been functioning correctly and was getting progressively worse.

Lisa had put herself on a percentage scale of 0 to 100, with zero representing suicide and 100% total health. The day I went to see her she was at ½%. As a nurse she had decided what drug to inject into her veins to end her life.

Our conversation revealed that she had been a very capable person, able to work, go to school, and still keep up with her home responsibilities.

Now she was at the point where even brushing her teeth took thought and effort. Certainly Satan had done his work well in stealing and destroying Lisa's potential.

I asked Lisa about reading the Bible and saying

affirmations, but she explained that her mind was not functioning well enough to comprehend what she was reading. So I promised that I would record some affirmations and scriptures on tape for her to listen to.

Within the next day or two, my husband and I went back to see Lisa and her husband. That day, after further counsel with Derin, he and I laid hands on Lisa and prayed for the healing of all the past hurts in her life, for forgiveness to flow through her to those who had hurt her, for freedom from fear in her life and also for physical healing.

Lisa's healing has been beautiful! Within two or three weeks she was reading whole books in a day. A short time later our Bible study class had a dinner together. Lisa did not bring her own special food that evening. She told the class that this was the first normal meal she'd eaten in over six years. She was elated, and so were we!

Within three months, Lisa was totally well. Spiritually, she was growing, reading the Word and Christian books and sharing God's love with others. Mentally, she was back to her past sharpness, able to grasp ideas and concepts with no problem.

Physically, she was healthy, eating everything she desired (and I mean everything!), and riding horseback. In fact, she no longer has an allergic reaction to anything and does not have to go to the doctor for allergy shots.

Lisa says she has discovered that there is life beyond the 100%. She feels she is more that totally healed now. She is joyful and vibrant and loving life.

Later Lisa moved to Seattle with her husband. Last fall they were back in Ft. Collins to attend a wedding.

Lisa was beautiful and radiantly healthy. She and her husband are active in a growing vital church and are counselors to those who want to accept Christ at their church meetings.

Lisa is again working, taking care of premature babies in a large hospital. She prays for the little ones she cares for, and has seen blindness, deafness, and brain damage healed. The doctors have said of the change in some of those for whom she has prayed, "This is a miracle!"

Before we prayed for Lisa, people had told her that it was God's will that she suffer. Praise the Lord, we didn't accept Satan's lie and let him destroy her life! Her testimony and abundant life bring glory to God.

I could relate several other stories about physical healings we've seen, but it is not the encouragement you receive in seeing others healed that heals you. Your own healing must come because of your faith in God and the infallibility of His Word.

My son, pay attention to what I say; listen closely to my words. Do not let them out of your sight, keep them within your heart; for they are life to those who find them and health to a man's whole body (Prov. 4:20-22).

The steps to health for the "whole body" are in these verses. First, give attention to God's Word, really *hear* it. Secondly, keep His words always before you, see yourself in your imagination as healed and whole. Thirdly, keep the Word in your heart through memorization and meditation.

Then the promise of Jeremiah 30:17 is yours: *"...I will restore you to health and heal your wounds,"* declares the Lord.

Affirm Strength

If you have been ill for some time and are still weak, God will supply strength.

Affirm:

Christ within gives me strength for every situation.

Confess:

I can do all things through Him (Christ) *who strengthens me* (Phil. 4:13 *NAS*).

But those who hope in the Lord will renew their strength (Is. 40:31).

I pray that out of his glorious riches he (God) *may strengthen you with power through his Spirit in your inner being* (Eph. 3:16).

For the eyes of the Lord range throughout the earth to strengthen those whose hearts are fully committed to him (2 Chron. 16:9).

It is not unusual, in our ministry, for me to minister to people in intercessory prayer and counsel for long hours at a time, or to be up very late at night in our teaching meetings. The result is that the next morning I am very tired.

Usually, that day I will have much work that needs to be done, and sometimes I feel too tired to do it. I have found that saying these verses on strength really works. When I say them, I come to the end of the day with the work accomplished and strengh left over. I am *strengthened with all power according to his glorious might so that* (I) *may have great endurance...* (Col. 1:11).

Prayer

"Father, I thank You that through Jesus, Your living Word, You have provided healing for my body

as well as my spirit.

"I choose today to walk in the divine health You have provided. My body is the temple of Your Holy Spirit. Reveal to me what that really means. Establish the truth of Your words within me for they are life to me and health to my whole body according to Proverbs 4:21.

"In the strong Name of Jesus, Amen."

11
FINANCIAL FREEDOM

Prosperity is another area in which you will find much doubt, a great deal of discussion, and a variety of beliefs among Christians.

If Christians do not know God's will for them in regard to their finances, if they don't believe it is His desire for His children to prosper, then they will usually suffer financial problems.

Certainly, Satan does not want us to prosper. The testimony of Christians having all they needed plus extra to give generously to others (as the Word promises in 2 Corinthians 9:8) would be so powerful in this world in which "money talks," that Satan knows our prosperity would be a major defeat for him. It would infuence even worldly people to take note, and we would have much more opportunity to witness to them that Jesus is Lord.

Satan wants the wealth of this earth to remain in the hands of the Mafia, illegal operators, pornographers, gamblers, the liquor industry and drug traffickers. Just think of the good all this money could do in the world if it were in the hands of believers who would use it as God directed them! Very quickly the Gospel could be taken to "all nations." It must bring Satan great delight when we keep confessing that poverty is good for Christians (because it keeps them humble!).

The Bible, God's written will for man, contains an abundance of scriptures which testify to us that God wants His children prosperous. Third John 2, for example, tells us: *Beloved, I pray that you may prosper in every way and [that your body] may keep well, even as [I know] your soul keeps well and prospers (AMP).*

Note that this verse says "prosper in every way." Certainly *in every way* must mean financially too!

First Corinthians 1:30 says, *Jesus is made unto us wisdom (KJV);* and Proverbs 8:18 says that with wisdom *are riches and honor, enduring wealth and prosperity.*

Psalm 35:27 tells us: *...say continually, Let the Lord be magnified, Who takes pleasure in the prosperity of His servant (AMP).* And since Jesus died and arose we are not merely servants of God, we are sons of God. Would He want His servants to be prosperous, but not His sons? Hardly!

Any doubts left? Read the blessings and curses found in Deuteronomy 28 and realize that *Christ purchased our freedom (redeeming us) from the curse..., by [Himself] becoming a curse for us, for it is written..., Cursed is everyone who hangs on a tree (is crucified); To the end that through [their receiving] Christ Jesus, the blessing [promised] to Abraham might come upon the Gentiles* (Gal. 3:13-14 *AMP).* Please note that one of Abraham's blessings was financial prosperity.

Why then are so many Christians in distressful financial circumstances? Because they have confessed, with their mouths, lack, and have believed (because of false teaching) in their hearts that God doesn't want them wealthy!

Ever heard a Christian say, "There is just never enough money to go around"; "We are always a few dollars short"; "We can't afford to tithe!"; or, "In today's economy it's just impossible to get ahead!"?

Confess Abundance

We must quit confessing lack! Instead, confess this affirmation:

I confess and accept God's financial blessings on our family (me). Each day our (my) needs are met.

For you know the grace of our Lord Jesus Christ, that through he was rich, yet for your sakes he became poor, so that you through his poverty might become rich (2 Cor. 8:9).

And God is able to make all grace abound to you, so that in all things at all times, having all that you need, you will abound in every good work (2 Cor. 9:8).

And my God will meet all your needs according to his glorious riches in Christ Jesus (Phil. 4:19).

Prosperity Pleases God

Some people say, "Yes, I can believe God will give us enough money for our actual needs; but I don't feel I can expect Him to give us more that that." Consider these verses:

You (Lord) still the hunger of those you cherish; their sons have plenty, and they store up wealth for their children (Ps. 17:14).

But remember the Lord your God, for it is he who gives you the ability to produce wealth, and so confirms his covenant, which he swore to your forefathers, as it is today (Deut. 8:18).

Christ warned against the love of money, putting it first, desiring it more than righteousness. Usually people who do not have enough money spend more time thinking about dollars and desiring (loving) them than the people who have plenty.

Dollars, or things, must not become our priority. We must always know that God — not banks, nor the economy, nor our employment — is our source of true riches.

If you are short of funds and/or in debt, affirm this:

We are (I am) debt free and know how to live in prosperity to the praise and glory of God.

Confess:

"Your beginnings will seem humble, so prosperous will your future be" (Job 8:7).

Remember me, O Lord, when you show favor to your people... that I may enjoy the prosperity of your chosen ones (Ps. 106:4-5).

He who did not spare his own Son, but gave him up for us all — how will he not also, along with him, graciously give us all things? (Rom. 8:32).

Blessed are all who fear the Lord, who walk in his ways. You will eat the fruit of your labor; blessings and prosperity will be yours (Ps. 128:1-2).

It is not always easy to stand firm in a confession. For my husband and me the area of finance has often been a difficult one. In 1981 Satan was able to cause us to lose our home and all the equity in it, but even then we continued to confess the verses I've shared with you concerning prosperity.

Here is the story of how God provided a very nice home for us at a time when it seemed we should be giving up all hope.

The Miracle House

In the summer of 1981 God miraculously provided a house for our family.

In the years from 1977 to 1981 we had lived in four different houses. So when we found out in the spring of 1981 that we would have to leave the house in which we were living, you can understand why I wasn't too happy about moving again.

Therefore, when a man from Oklahoma told us that God had directed him to buy us a home, we were overjoyed. We found a house that was right for us and in the correct price range for him, and the arrangements were made.

But about a month later, after we were all moved into the house, Mr. Long called to say he could not get his assets in order and would not be able to come up with the agreed financing to buy us the house.

Satan started mocking me as I cleaned, washed curtains and windows, weeded the flower gardens, hung pictures, and did all those things one does to make a house a home. He said, ''Why are you doing all this work when you'll have to move out right away?''

But my husband and I made a quality decision. We decided that Mr. Long was not our source, God was. We would depend on God to meet our needs!

Over the past few years I have found out the best way to stand against Satan is to use God's Word. So it was no surprise when I felt directed to read in the book of Nehemiah where God showed me this verse: *...they took possession of houses filled with all kinds of good things, wells already dug, vineyards, ...and fruit trees in abundance. ...they revelled in your great goodness* (Nem. 9:25).

After that, whenever Satan would try to tempt me to fear I would quote that verse and/or some other verses on homes and provision that I found in the Word.

When the day for the closing on the house came,

we still had no money at all to pay the owners of the house. At the closing my husband stated our position. We were standing in faith that God would provide the money needed to pay for the house.

In the eyes of the world going to a house closing with no money is very foolish and we met with some rather severe persecution. But God had assured us in our spirits that He would provide.

From the world's point of view we should have immediately packed up and moved out, but whenever I would think about packing, that inner voice in my spirit would say, "Rita, this is your house, you don't have to move." So I never did pack, not even one box.

Instead I acted in faith and hung up a new picture! I spent time in God's Word. I confessed scriptures about His provision. We "rechecked" with our spiritual counselors who assured us we were to "stay put." So for ten long days we did.

I was reading, in my morning devotional times, in First and Second Corinthians and writing down the verse or verses that impressed me each day. When I looked back on these verses "after the fact" I knew that God had directed! Here are the verses and the dates they were given to me:

Aug. 21: Therefore, my dear brothers, stand firm. Let nothing move you. Always give yourselves fully to the work of the Lord, because you know your labor in the Lord is not in vain (1 Cor. 15:58). *...it is by faith you stand firm* (2 Cor. 1:24).

This was the day, a Friday, that we received a notice to appear in court.

Aug. 22: I noted these verses. We are hard pressed on every side, but not crushed; perplexed, but not in despair;

persecuted, but not abandoned; struck down, but not destroyed (2 Cor. 4:8-9). *...we have a building from God, an eternal house in heaven, not built by human hands* (2 Cor. 5:1).

This day was probably the one when I was the most tempted to doubt. The court order had been delivered by the sheriff's department and contained charges against us and a demand for $145.00 per day for each day we remained in the house. Still I did not pack because my spirit was not released to do so.

Aug. 23: ...now is the time of God's favor, now is the day of salvation (2 Cor. 6:2).

That day a lady, whom we didn't even know, but who knew of our situation, said to a mutual friend of ours: "It's too bad the Carmacks have already moved. If they hadn't moved we could have helped them."

Our friend replied, "But they haven't moved!"

At this point, the lady and her husband came to us and informed us that they would buy the house for us because the Holy Spirit had told them to. They said they could get the cash the next day.

That next morning, August 24, the verses I read were for our benefactors, Mr. and Mrs. James: *This service that you perform is not only supplying the needs of God's people but is also overflowing in many expressions of thanks to God. Because of the service by which you have proved yourselves, men will praise God for... (your) obedience..., and for your generosity...* (2 Cor. 9:12-13).

God kept His promise to us: *My people will live in peaceful dwelling places, in secure homes, in undisturbed places of rest* (Is. 32:18). Mr. and Mrs. James said the Holy Spirit had directed them to provide the money for our home. As I write this I praise the Lord that, for the first summer in five years, I do not have to move! God's Word is true, I have a secure home.

Now a word of caution! I have seen so many Christians who are gullible in the area of finances. The Word says that with *wisdom* are found riches and honor, enduring wealth and prosperity. (Prov. 8:18.)

Too often all a ''con artist'' has to say is that his company is Christian and that their one goal in life is to help Christians make lots of money to give to their church. Many times that is all it takes to influence Christians to part with their hard-earned money, only to discover later that all those rosy success stories of people making thousands were very isolated cases or not true at all. Some people only learn the hard way that ''get-rich-quick schemes'' are not good Christian stewardship!

If you have been foolish in business deals or have had poor habits in handling money, you need to start with this affirmation:

Because I am a good steward of God's resources, He can trust me with abundance. I have financial wisdom.

Confess these verses:

''You have been faithful in a few things; I will put you in charge of many things'' (Matt. 25:21).

If any of you lacks wisdom, he should ask of God, who gives generously to all..., and it will be given to him (James 1:5).

...Christ Jesus ...has become for us wisdom from God (1 Cor. 1:30).

In everything you do, put God first, and he will direct you and crown your efforts with success (Prov. 3:6 *TLB*).

(Also use Proverbs 8:18 which is quoted earlier.)

There is much in the Bible concerning sowing and reaping, giving and receiving, and harvesting. If you are a farmer or a gardener, you will understand this principle.

When I plant a garden each spring I *fully* expect a good return! For one kernel of corn I expect two or three ears with many, many kernels on them. How many times larger is a full-grown carrot that the tiny carrot seed planted in the ground? Probably thousands of times! Or what about the return on one zucchini squash seed? Tremendous! We serve the God of goodness and bounty!

We need to carry this same kind of belief over into the area of giving and receiving in finances. This affirmation and these verses will help establish expectancy for a good harvest from your Father:

I believe in God's laws of sowing and reaping. I expect a good and bountiful harvest.

"As long as the earth endures, seedtime and harvest, ...will never cease" (Gen. 8:22).

For the Lord your God will bless you in all your harvest and in all the work of your hands, and your joy will be complete (Deut. 16:15).

...he who sows righteousness reaps a sure reward (Prov. 11:18).

...the seed on good soil stands for those with a noble and good heart, who hear the word, retain it, and by persevering produce a crop (Luke 8:15).

Notice the words "by persevering." When I plant my garden in the spring, the first thing to come up is weeds. So I wait and in a few days radishes, onions and peas appear. But I have to wait still longer before these tiny plants mature and are ready to harvest.

I don't go out three days after I've planted the seeds and say, ''I guess God's law about planting and reaping just doesn't work for me.'' No, I spend time; first waiting, then weeding and watering — then the harvest comes.

I challenge you to spend as much time planting the Word, weeding (pulling out doubts and negative words), and watering (meditating and praying) in your life for the next 120 days (about the average time it takes a garden to fully mature) as you would to grow a vegetable garden. You will see a harvest! God's Word will not return empty. (Is. 55:11.)

Last summer we had a severe hail and wind storm. My garden looked hopeless! But I didn't go out and plow it all under. I pulled off the dead parts, propped the plants back up, and cultivated the hard, crusty ground. (I also prayed for resurrection!) By August people were amazed at the large healthy plants in my garden.

Don't let Satan's storms defeat you. *Persevere* in prayer and in speaking the Word!

Prayer

''Lord, I open up my mind to receive the truth in Your Word concerning finances. Help me to realize that it is Your will that I have financial freedom and be prosperous.

''I pledge myself to be a good steward of the money that flows into my hands, and I will give freely to God's work so that the Gospel can go out and bring men to salvation and healing.

''In Jesus' Name, Amen.''

12

FREEDOM TO BELIEVE

Next to love, faith is probably the most often used theme in sermons. The Bible says that without faith it is impossible to please God. (Heb. 11:6.) When a person accepts Christ, he is given a measure of faith, so all Christians have faith to a certain extent.

Many times Christians are praying for more faith when what they really need is more knowledge and understanding! — knowledge of God's will and His ways as found in His Word; understanding of the nature and character of God and of our rights and privileges as His children.

God's Love

We first need to establish deep within our spirit that God really does love us. Individually. Unconditionally. Lavishly. Forever.

God wants us to comprehend, as much as is humanly possible, this love. In Ephesians 3:17-19 Paul says, *And I pray that you, being rooted and established in love, may have power, ...to grasp how wide and long and high and deep is the love of Christ, and to know this love that surpasses knowledge.*

You see, Satan is always trying to deceive us and blind us to God's love because he knows that everyone who really understands how much God loves him will gladly serve God, giving his life and love to Him.

Often, even those who are serving and loving God still need help in knowing His love and forgiveness toward them. This is especially true if their earthly father did not express much love toward them.

This affirmation will help you comprehend God's love toward you, His child!

My spirit and mind are always aware that God, my Father, loves me unconditionally.

How great is the love the Father has lavished on us, that we should be called children of God! (1 John 3:1).

"I (God) have loved you with an everlasting love; I have drawn you with loving-kindness" (Jer. 31:3).

...put your hope in the Lord, for with the Lord is unfailing love and with him is full redemption (Ps. 130:7).

And the Lord has declared this day that you are his people, his treasured possession... (Deut. 26:18).

For I am convinced that... (nothing) *...in all creation, will be able to separate us from the love of God...* (Rom. 8:38-39).

God's Protection

Because God loves us so much He watches over us — much as a mother watches over and protects her small children.

It is my understanding that in the animal kingdom the only mothers that do not run from fires and leave their young behind are those of the chicken family.

Isn't it interesting that Satan has caused us to commonly use the word "chicken" to denote cowardly behavior, when really chickens are so brave?

In Psalm 91:4 we read: *He (God) will cover you with his feathers, and under his wings you will find refuge.*

When Jesus was lamenting over Jerusalem, He said, *"...how often I have longed to gather your children together, as a hen gathers her chicks under her wings, but you were not willing!"* (Luke 13:34).

God's illustration was based on truth. The truth of sacrificial love that is "willing to lay down its life" for another.

These verses on protection are ones I use on a regular basis. They cast out fear when my children are away from me. As I say them, I open an avenue so that God can send angels to protect me and my loved ones.

Affirm:

God's protection always surrounds my family and me.

Confess:

If you make the Most High your dwelling — even the Lord, ...then no harm will befall you, no disaster will come near your tent. For he will command his angels concerning you to guard you in all your ways (Ps. 91:9-11).

(The entire Ninety-First Psalm is excellent for illustrating God's protection.)

Spread your protection over them, that those who love your name may rejoice in you. For surely, O Lord, you bless the righteous; you surround them with your favor as with a shield (Ps. 5:11-12).

The children of Your servants shall dwell safely... (Ps. 102:28 *AMP*).

...you have ten thousand guardians in Christ... (1 Cor. 4:15).

Have you ever heard someone say, "I just knew something bad was going to happen," or has someone ever told you about a bad dream that "came true"?

In Agnes Sanford's book, *The Healing Light*,[9] she explains that this is God's way of warning us of

[9]Logos International, Plainfield, N.J., 1972

impending danger or tragedy. If we will learn to use that warning as a call to prayer we can avoid the tragic situation.

Lately this happened to me. My married daughter and her husband decided to go to a Christian concert in Denver on New Year's Eve. There had been a storm in Denver the week before and I had heard many reports about how bad the roads and streets were there. Also I knew that there are many people who drink and drive on New Year's Eve.

These thoughts made me have some concern about their going, but my husband said I shouldn't try to talk them out of it since they were adults and able to make their own decision.

Nevertheless my spirit was quite troubled, more than is usual for me over this type of situation. So throughout that day I prayed ''in the spirit'' and in English for their protection and I spoke protection for them using God's Word.

They went to Denver and the concert, and late that night as they were driving home they decided to get off the interstate highway and stop for a cup of coffee. As they were driving down the off-ramp, away from the heavy flow of traffic, the brakes on their car suddenly failed completely. There was a deep snow bank on that ramp so Peter just headed the car into it and they stopped—entirely safely!

They even ''happened'' to have $35 cash along, so they had the money they needed to stay in a motel that night. The next morning my husband went down and rescued their old Nova and brought them home.

What would have happened had I not prayed? I can't really say. I'm just thankful I knew to pray instead of ignoring God's "hunch"! In answer to my prayers He gave His angels "charge over them"!

God's Comfort

Again this morning I dreamed about my mother and was sobbing and weeping in my sleep. It has been a little over a year since she died and still, at times, sorrow almost overwhelms me.

So many things remind me of her. So very often I want to share things with her. Beautiful clouds and sunsets, the flowers in my yard, the pink peony I picked just yesterday which came from a transplant from the large beautiful bed of peonies in her back yard. "Antiquing" is not half as much fun alone; how we used to enjoy showing each other the beautiful and unique things we saw in antique shops!

Ours was not the ordinary mother-daughter relationship. So deep was our love and understanding of each other, so kindred our spirits, that neither of us ever remembered having had a fight or serious disagreement. I often told her, "If I could have chosen any mother in the world, you are the one I would have picked."

I delighted in going to her house or having her come to visit me. I knew if I could only be the kind of mother she had been I would be raising my children right. I didn't live up to that. Mother was simply too wonderful — but there was and is a good, loving relationship between my children and me.

I could go on and on about her virtues, but I guess they could be summed up in the fruit of the Spirit as listed in Galations 5:22-23. She had a loving, peaceful, joyful spirit. She literally sang her way through my childhood days. (She had a beautiful voice and often sang at special occasions.) But she also sang many hymns as she did her daily work:

"God has not promised skies always blue,
Flower-strewn pathways, all my life through.
But God has promised strength for the day,
Help for the labor, light for the way..."

The list does not end there: "patience, kindness, goodness, faithfulness, gentleness, and self-control." All of these she possessed and displayed in her life.

As you can imagine then I was in great sorrow when Satan caused her death through cancer. Without my knowledge of God's love and comfort, and my understanding of His will for His beloved children, I don't know what I would have done.

But I can tell you what I did do, and was helped and comforted and healed through it. If you are experiencing grief right now, you too can use this to gain comfort and healing.

This is the statement I made:

"Lord, I yield up to You all the hurt, sorrow and grief in my life. I praise You that I no longer have to carry them because Jesus carried them for me."

Then I quoted scriptures such as:

He was... a man of sorrows, and familiar with suffering... Surely he took up our infirmities and carried our sorrows (Is. 53:3-4).

He has sent me to bind up the brokenhearted, ...to comfort all who mourn, and provide for those who grieve... to bestow on them... the oil of gladness instead of mourning, and a garment of praise instead of a spirit of despair (Is. 61:1-3).

Praise be to the God and Father of our Lord Jesus Christ, the Father of compassion and the God of all comfort, who comforts us in all our troubles (2 Cor. 1:3-4).

The Lord is close to the brokenhearted... (Ps. 34:18).

(There were many other verses I used. They are on the cards available through our ministry.)

Even as I read these words and have written them, once again I find the spirit of heaviness lifting and God bringing comfort to my heart. Truly He is a God of love and comfort!

God's Faithfulness

Now that we know about God's faithfulness and goodness to us, it is easier to have faith in Him.

Hebrews 11:6 says, *...without faith it is impossible to please God, because anyone who comes to him must believe that he exists and that he rewards those who earnestly seek him.*

"He rewards those who earnestly seek him." That means that He rewards you, for if you weren't an "earnest seeker" you would not have read this book through to this point!

That is why we need to know of God's love, protection, and comfort because now we can have faith that He is our "reward." It will now be easy to have faith in God's faithfulness.

Speaking in Faith

There is a story in 2 Kings 4 about a Shunammite woman and her son which illustrates this idea of speaking in faith. According to the Biblical acccount, the boy died, a fact of which the mother was well aware. Yet this woman, in faith, confessed first to her husband, *"It will be well"* (v. 23 *NAS*). Then she made the same confession to several specific questions asked her by Elisha's servant: *"It is well"* (v. 26 *NAS*). She acted in faith — confessing what she wanted and believed would be — and God, through Elisha, brought her son back to life.

Now this was before Romans 4:17 and 8:28 were written! Today we have Christ's life and words and the Holy Spirit's empowering to help us speak in faith.

I was reading Luke 17 one day and verses five and six impressed me in a new way: *The apostles said to the Lord, "Increase our faith!" He replied, "If you have faith as small as a mustard seed, you can say to this mulberry tree, 'Be uprooted and planted in the sea,' and it will obey you."*

We have concentrated too much attention on the "mustard seed" in those verses. I think Jesus was saying, "Don't worry about *how much* faith you have; even if it is infinitesimal, go ahead and act on it. Speak forth words that can used to change circumstances, to move immovable obstacles."

Jesus didn't say that the disciples needed more faith. He didn't tell them how to get more faith. He didn't offer to give them more faith. He didn't tell them to pray for more faith. He said, "Act on the faith you have. *Say* what you want and that will bring results." He knew the results they saw would increase their faith.

Is there any better way to have your faith increased than to see results from your prayers and from saying God's Word? The people with the strongest faith are those who have seen, personally, answers to their prayers because they stood firm, speaking forth God's

Word.

The world says, "Seeing is believing"; but God says, "Believing is seeing." In Romans 4:17 we find that God *calls things that are not as though they were.* That is what the Shunammite woman did when she said, *"Everything is all right"* (2 Kings 4:23), even though her son was dead and she knew it!

We can learn to see through spiritual eyes, then "know" in our spirit and thus *have the faith of God* (KJV), or in other words, have a God-kind of faith, as Jesus said to do in Mark 11:22.

God is our rewarder!

Prayer

"My Lord and my God, I cannot even express my praise that You are the great I AM and yet You love, protect, heal and comfort me!

"Establish a strong faith within me to take hold of the truth concerning Your character, Lord. Again, I pray that You help me comprehend, as much as humanly possible, Your love for me.

"Thank You for taking grief out of my heart. I praise You for taking doubt out of my mind. Thank You that I walk in Your love and protection at all times.

"I praise the Name of Jesus! Amen."

13
FREEDOM TO MATURE

There are many "spiritual exercises" we can do that will bring added maturity and depth to our Christian walk. Prayer and studying God's Word are probably the two most obvious. My ideas on making the Word a very real part of our inner being and using it every day, becoming a "doer of the Word," are contained in the last chapter of this book. So now let's look at prayer.

Positive Praying

There are many books that are entirely devoted to the subject of prayer and intercession. So there is much instruction available to you in ths area.

Therefore I will only share briefly some ideas that I haven't read much about in the usual books on prayer.

If you are like I used to be, you pray silently except when leading in prayer at a public service or prayer meeting. Try praying aloud in your private devotions. It will help keep your mind from wandering and it is something you can do while driving the car or doing housework.

The other thing that's changed for me is how I pray for people's needs. I suppose this can best be illustrated through examples:

Before: "Dear Lord, please help _____ to quit cheating on his wife and come back to You."
Now:"Dear Lord, I bless _____ with a new love for his wife. I bless him with a thirst for righteousness

and a longing to be in a right relationship with You.''

Before: ''Dear Lord, please heal _____ of her cancer. Help the terrible pain to go away!'' *Now:* ''Dear Lord, I bless _____ today with Your strength and with health. I bless her with comfort and a warm sense of Your presence.''

Before: ''Dear Lord, I can't stand the way my kids are fighting. Help them to quit being so naughty!'' *Now:* ''Dear Lord, I bless my children with a spirit of love and cooperation toward each other. I bless them with good attitudes and a willingness to obey and do right.''

The first kind of prayer presents the problem. You ''see'' the problem in your mind as you send it up to God. The second kind of prayer ''sees'' the answer to the problem and positive results are portrayed. To me the way I pray now is a faith way of praying, ''calling things that are not as though they were.'' (Rom. 4:17.)

I practiced this ''visualizing'' in my prayers for a friend of ours who had suffered a very serious back injury. He had been through many operations and was in constant severe pain. As I prayed for him, I ''saw'' him doing the activities he had enjoyed before the injury such as bowling and playing volleyball. Now he is completely healed and we've been bowling with him and his wife. The visualization became reality.

The name of another lady, whom I've still never met, was given to me as a prayer request by a friend of mine who is a nurse. This lady had a serious disease which had paralyzed her whole body. When I went to town I drove by her house so I could visualize her healed, standing in the door waving to her husband as he went out to work in their farm fields. My nurse friend kept reporting to me about how Eileen was getting better and better until she was completely well and able to go home from the hospital. **Seeing your answer as you pray is praying in faith!**

There are two more ways of praying that are very effective. One is in tongues, letting the Holy Spirit pray through you, about a situation or person. This way you know you are praying God's will because the Holy Spirit would never contradict God.

The other way is praying the Word. For example:

"Father, I thank You that You have given Your angels charge over me to keep me in all my ways (Ps. 91:11.), and that You surround me with Your favor as with a shield. (Ps. 5:12.)

"I praise You for sending Your Word and healing me (Ps. 107:20.), and that You keep me free from every disease. (Deut. 7:15)

"I thank You that the fruit of the Spirit of love, joy, peace, patience, kindness, goodness, faithfulness, gentleness and self-control are operating in my life. (Gal. 5:22-23.)

"I praise You for making me Your child and lavishing Your love upon me. (1 John 3:1.)"

Again, you know you are praying correctly when you pray God's Word because His word is His will.

The "thirst for righteousness" prayer (Matt. 5:6.) is a great one to use for the unsaved or for someone who is not walking in God's will. For about a year I prayed this prayer for a relative of mine. The next time we saw him he was very open to spiritual things and let Derin pray and counsel with him. Today he is completely changed and has grown so much spiritually. Before, there was virtually no communication between us. Now there is a beautiful relationship. **Praying the Word works!**

Here is an affirmation and some verses on prayer:

I have a fulfilling prayer life. Communication with God is a delight to me.

Do not be anxious about anything, but in everything, by prayer and petition, with thanksgiving, present your requests to God. And the peace of God, which transcends all understanding, will guard your hearts and your minds in Christ Jesus (Phil. 4:6-7).

Let us then approach the throne of grace with confidence, so that we may receive mercy and find grace to help us in our time of need (Heb. 4:16).

"I tell you the truth, my Father will give you whatever you ask in my name... Ask and you will receive, and your joy will be complete" (John 16:23-24).

This is the assurance we have in approaching God: that if we ask anything according to his will, he hears us. And if we know that he hears us — whatever we ask — we know that we have what we asked of him (1 John 5:14-15).

(See also Matthew 6:5-13 where Christ is instructing His disciples on how to pray, giving them the example of the Lord's Prayer.)

Notice again that prayer results in answers and blessings from God. When you see these results in your life you will be encouraged in your prayer life so that it becomes a delight to you.

Remember, when you pray, see through the problem to the reality of Christ and His answers!

Power in Praise

The Bible is filled with praise and thanksgiving to God. God wants and needs our praise. Praise releases Him to work on our behalf.

Praise lifts burdens, cures depression and glorifies God.

Affirm:

Praise and thankfulness to God are a daily part of my life.

I will praise you, O Lord, with all my heart; I will tell of all your wonders. I will be glad and rejoice in you; I will sing praise to your name, O Most High (Ps. 9:1-2).

Praise the Lord, O my soul; all my inmost being, praise his holy name. Praise the Lord, O my soul, and forget not all his benefits (Ps. 103:1-2).

...give thanks in all circumstances, for this is God's will for you in Christ Jesus (1 Thess. 5:18).

Sing and make music in your heart to the Lord, always giving thanks to God the Father for everything, in the name of our Lord Jesus Christ (Eph. 5:19-20).

I will extol the Lord at all times: his praise will always be on my lips (Ps. 34:1).

O Lord, open my lips, and my mouth will declare your praise (Ps. 51:15).

Through Jesus, therefore, let us continually offer to God a sacrifice of praise — the fruit of lips that confess his name (Heb. 13:15).

Integrate Praise

I often felt that I did not praise God enough. I usually started my prayer time with praise, and some days I offered up praises at various moments during the day. Certainly God did not get the volume of praise I felt He desired from me. I did not live up to the verse, *His praise shall continually be in my mouth* (Ps. 34:1 *AMP*).

I've found that I can praise God in conjuction with my affirmations. I've discovered that this way the affirmations become even more meaningful and take on new power and inspiration for me.

I will give you an example of how I do this:

"Lord, I praise You that Jesus' light is in me, completely healing my spirit, mind and body.

"I praise You that by Jesus' wounds I am healed. (1 Pet. 2:24.) Jesus, I thank You that You took up my diseases and carried my illnesses. (Matt. 8:17.) Lord, I thank You that You sent Your Word and healed me. (Ps. 107:20.) I praise You, God, that Your words are life and health to my whole body. (Prov. 4:22.)

***"Praise the Lord, O my soul... He... heals all my diseases* (Ps. 103:2-3).**

"I praise You, Lord, that You give me a full life span (Ex. 23:26.), and that I will go to the grave in full vigor. (Job 5:26.) Praise the Lord."

Re-read my example right now, out loud, and see how it lifts your spirit and quickens your faith. When you praise, your affirmations will have double impact. You will grow even faster in your areas of affirmation. Praise will become an exciting and joyous thing in your life!

Worshipping God

Praise and worship to God and his Son, Jesus, are often looked upon as one and the same. To me there is a difference between the two. I see worship as a more quiet, adoration-type prayer.

In listening to a sermon by Norvel Hayes my conscience was pricked because I so seldom bowed down on my knees and just spent time giving love, worship, adoration and thanksgiving to God. Since hearing Brother Hayes I have started doing this and have found it very meaningful to me.

I have been kneeling and praying and praising God out loud, for several minutes at a time, just worshipping and thanking Him for who He is, for His Son Jesus, and for the Holy Spirit. I thank Him for His love for me and express my love for Him.

I often end this time of worship by praying the Lord's Prayer or the first five verses of Psalm 103. I am sure that if you will do this, it will be a real blessing to you too.

I also highly recommend that you read a book by Anne Murchison entitled *Praise and Worship (on Earth as It is in Heaven)*.[10] This book beautifully explains how and why we should worship God in singing, clapping and dancing. Reading it has inspired me to be more expressive in my praise and worship to God.

Prayer

"Lord, teach me to pray prayers that You can answer, prayers that are in Your will, prayers that are powerful to the pulling down of Satan's strongholds,

[10]Word Books, Waco, Texas, 1981

prayers that are full of faith and single-minded in purpose.

"Help me to learn to praise and worship You in spirit and in truth! Lift me out of the confining traditions of men and help me soar freely to the heights of Your holy joy!

"In praise and worship to the Holy Name of Jesus, Amen."

14
FREEDOM THROUGH THE WORD

I am glad that you made it through to this last chapter because, in many ways, it is the key to making the whole idea of this book work!

To some of the groups in which I've taught I've posed these questions:

"How many of you believe that God's Word has the answers to your problems?"

Usually people are very affirmative about this. They believe that the Bible has the answers they need.

I then instruct them to think about a problem area in their life — the thing which Satan uses most often to trip them up.

Then my last question is:

"How many verses of scripture have you memorized that you can instantly quote to defeat Satan in that area?"

The room always becomes very quiet after that!

My husband has even gone so far as to ask people in the audience to raise their hand if they know two or three verses they can quote on healing, or prosperity, or protection. In the average group of Christians there are very few hands raised — perhaps five out of 100!

God says in Hosea 4:6: *"My people are destroyed from lack of knowledge."*

We say, "He was such a good Christian. How could God let such a terrible thing happen to him?"

God didn't "let it happen"! Every day good Christians are "being destroyed" by Satan because they lack knowledge of God's will and God's Word.

When He was tempted in the wilderness, Christ quoted scripture in answer to Satan's suggestions. (Matt. 4:1-11.) Three times Jesus said, *"It is written."* (vs. 4,7,10.) Jesus used the Word to overcome Satan. We must follow His example!

God's Word is true. Satan is a liar, but even he knows that the Word is true. We win over Satan by knowing the truth in the Bible.

Meditate on the Word

Meditation is most effectively done with scripture that is memorized. Note, in the following verses, the benefits or rewards of meditation: defense against sin, answered prayer, prosperity, success, and health.

I have hidden your word in my heart that I might not sin against you (Ps. 119:11).

"If you remain in me (Jesus) *and my words remain in you, ask whatever you wish, and it will be given you"* (John 15:7).

"Do not let this Book of the Law depart from your mouth; meditate on it day and night, so that you may be careful to do everything written in it. Then you will be prosperous and successful" (Josh. 1:8).

...his (the righteous man's) *delight is in the law of the Lord, and on his law he meditates day and night... Whatever he does prospers* (Ps. 1:2-3).

He sent forth his word and healed them (Ps. 107:20).

The power of the Word is released on our behalf when we know it, say it, do it and use it in our daily lives.

Satan may have you thinking, "But I just can't memorize God's Word." That is a deceitful lie! Do you know your name, address, and phone number? Then you can remember Bible verses!

Make this affirmation:

It is easy for me to memorize the Word of God. I have it deep in my heart to use every day. It gives me victory over temptation.

Virtually all of Psalm 119 is about the Word, and it is the longest chapter in the whole Bible. Read it and choose some verses from it to quote as you make the above affirmation.

I especially like these verses:

Verse 11: *I have hidden your word in my heart that I might not sin against you.*

Verse 13: *With my lips I recount all the laws that come from your mouth.*

Verse 37: *Turn my eyes away from worthless things; renew my life according to your word.*

Verses 65-66: *Do good to your servant according to your word, O Lord. Teach me knowledge and good judgment, for I believe in your commands.*

Verse 165: *Great peace have they who love your law, and nothing can make them stumble.*

If you are more familiar with other translations, such as the *King James Version* or the *New American Standard Bible*, look up in them the verses I've suggested and memorize them. You should have at least three verses memorized for each of your affirmations so that whenever Satan tempts you in that area you can immediately quote scripture to him. *Resist the devil, and he will flee from you* (James 4:7). Quoting scripture is your best form of resistance!

In Jeremiah 1:12 God assures us, *"...I am watching to see that my word is fulfilled."*

In Colossians 3:16 we are told, *Let the word of Christ dwell in you richly...* with the results being wisdom and gratitude.

We cannot take this admonition lightly. For Christian maturity and God's blessings we must memorize His Word!

Use the Word

I know these methods work, because I have been using them for almost five years now.

In the fall and winter of 1980-81 our family was going through a very difficult time. My mother was very ill, needing constant care. Our unmarried teenaged daughter was pregnant, and our house was being sold by the former owner because we could not come up with a large payment we owed him, leaving us without any equity.

In the past my heart would have been burdened and sad over any one of these situations alone. Depression, frustration and anger would have been my natural reaction.

But, for the two and one half years before all this happened I had been practicing what I've "preached" in this book. So I knew what to do. I confessed I had hope, wisdom, joy and peace. And that is what God enabled me to have — in spite of the traumatic circumstances.

I'm not saying I was never discouraged or distressed, but I am saying that God and His Word helped me to be victorious over Satan. I never once had to resort to sleeping pills, Valium or Maalox to help me "cope" with the problems.

The answers in this book have also helped me be able to reach out and effectively help others who are hurting. I have a new boldness to witness and lead others to salvation. People are healed when I pray for their physical bodies. But most rewarding of all is the hope and joy I see in other Christians' eyes when I confirm that what they had hoped all along is true; that God's Word does have what they need; that Jesus can heal their inner being so they can be free of fear, inferiority, depression, guilt and anger; and that the Holy Spirit will empower them to be "more than conquerors" in their life!

I pray that this book has helped you understand, in a practical way, how you can *say* answers and *see* answers, instead of problems, in your life.

Jesus once said of a certain group in His day: *"...this people's heart has become calloused; they hardly hear with their ears, and they have closed their eyes. Otherwise they might see with their eyes, hear with their ears, understand with their hearts, and turn, and I would heal them"* (Matt. 13:15).

I pray that this may never be true of you, but rather that you will take these principles from the Word of God and apply them to your life so that Christ may say of you: *"But blessed are your eyes because they see, and your ears because they hear"* (v. 16).

Prayer

"Lord God, Author of all Truth, I come to You and ask that the Word come alive in me. I will be a doer of the Word and not a hearer only. I will hide

Your Word in my heart. I will meditate on it day and night.

"I will know the Truth and the Truth will set me free. Your Word is Truth. Help it to saturate my spirit and mind completely.

"Thank You, Lord, that Your Word became flesh and dwelt among us!

"It is in His Name, Jesus, that I pray. Amen."

ABOUT THE AUTHOR

Rita Carmack's love for people has led her into ministry to those who are discouraged and hurting. For five years she and her husband, Derin, have had a teaching ministry. Rita also appears frequently on the live call-in radio broadcast of "Derin's Coffee Shop" which is produced daily for one hour at 1:00 p.m. Eastern time on the Satellite Radio Network. (If your Christian radio station doesn't broadcast this program, call the station and request that it be carried. Ask the station to contact "Derin's Coffee Shop" at (303) 226-5911, and a demonstration tape will be sent.)

Rita was an elementary teacher for several years. Today, she is a wife, mother and grandmother. Her interests include writing, reading, teaching, gardening and antiques.

ADDITIONAL MATERIALS AVAILABLE

Additional copies of this book may be ordered for $5.00 per copy.

A complete set of affirmations on pocket-size cards is available for a cost of $2.00.

Teaching tapes by Rita Carmack may be ordered from the list below. Each single tape is $5.00.

____ **How the Word Gave Me Hope** (personal testimony)
____ **Confessing Healing**
____ **Becoming a Congruent Person**
____ **The Transforming Power of the Word**
____ **Walking in the Word** (Derin and Rita)
____ **Renewing the Mind**
____ **Praying the Word**
____ **Praying with Confidence**
____ **Marriage and Family** (2 tapes — $10.00)
    (or may be ordered separately as:)
____   **The Renewed Marriage**
____   **Raising Children in God's Ways**
Orders should be sent to:

Jewel Communications International, Inc.
4836 South College Avenue
Fort Collins, CO 80525